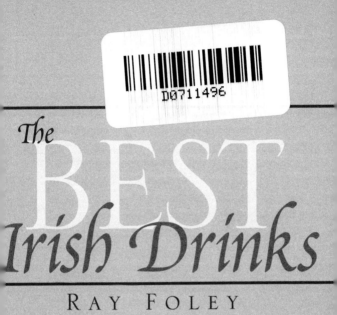

The BEST Irish Drinks

RAY FOLEY

SOURCEBOOKS, INC.
NAPERVILLE, ILLINOIS

Published by Sourcebooks, Inc.
P.O. Box 4410, Naperville, Illinois 60567-4410
(630) 961-3900
FAX: (630) 961-2168
www.sourcebooks.com

Library of Congress Cataloging-in-Publication Data
Foley, Ray.
  [Spirits of Ireland]
  The best Irish drinks / Ray Foley.
    p. cm.
  Originally published: The spirits of Ireland. [United States] : Foley Pub., c1998.
  ISBN-13: 978-1-4022-0678-8
  ISBN-10: 1-4022-0678-X
  1. Cocktails. 2. Bartending. 3. Alcoholic beverages—Ireland. I. Title.

TX951.F594 2006
641.8'7409417—dc22

                                                                2005025015

Printed and bound in Canada.
WC 10 9 8 7 6 5 4 3 2 1

DEDICATION

To John J. Foley Sr. (limerick), Ellen Josephine (Russell) Foley (Tipperary), and Ryan Peter Foley, a great Irish American.

TABLE OF CONTENTS

Introduction

ACKNOWLEDGMENTS

To all the suppliers who came forth with information on their products:

Heineken USA

Brown-Forman Beverage Co.

C&C International, Ltd.

A. Hardy USA, Ltd.

Whitehall Advertising

IDV North America

Guinness Import Co.

Nancy Larkin, Camelot

Heaven Hill Distilleries, Inc.

Vince Piscopo, Wells, Rich, Greene

Stephen Davis, Heineken USA

John Vidal, Anita Galvin, Brown-Forman Beverage Co.

Alan Lewis, C&C International, Ltd.

William J. Walsh, A. Hardy USA, Ltd.

Patricia Bornmann, Whitehall Advertising

Michael L. Avitable, Marie Brizard Wines & Spirits USA

Meg Syberg, David Sherman Corp.

Howard Pulchin, Guinness Import Company

Barry Berish, Michael Donahue, Jim Beam Brands Co.

Jim Cotter, Stephen L. Kauffman, Susan Overton, Heaven Hill Distilleries, Inc.

Katie Bush, Keith Steer, Halbleib/Beggs, Inc.

Mark Doyle, Austin, Nichols & Co., Inc.
The Milton Samuels Agency
Karen Danik, Cairns & Associates, Inc.

Plus, Jaclyn Wilson Foley for her loyalty, Loretta Natiello for being my best friend, J.K. for his assistance, and all the great Irish bars and bartenders who contributed to *Bartender* magazine with their great recipes.

INTRODUCTION

God gave the recipe for whiskey to the people of Ireland because he loved them. Among His treasures are a few that are exceedingly rare, and one of these is the Water of Life. "What better gift," He asked Himself one fine misty morning, "for these truly unusual and gifted people?" No wonder they call it spirit.

In his customary oblique manner, the Almighty did not simply appear by a Sligo bog one day with barley under one arm and an alembic under the other. He chose instead to instruct folks in a distant land—hazy references mention "the East," probably lands occupied by the Mohammedans—in the art of distillation. The stimulant of choice among these folks was coffee, and they never tried their hand at distilling grains. Theirs is the loss; they chose instead to distill fragrances.

It could have been any monk, or group of monks, but some of the old folks insist it was St. Patrick who pocketed the formula for distillation on a visit to the East and returned with it to the Emerald Isle in the fifth century. Born in Britain, Patrick was captured and taken to Ireland as a slave at age sixteen. He escaped six years later, wandered around the continent, and eventually took holy orders. The record of his visit to the East is missing, but he might have been among those Christians who travelled to the land of the infidel to spread the gospel. In any event, he returned to Ireland, thrust himself and the teachings of the Roman church upon the king at Tara, gave the snakes their marching orders, and set up the first pot still. What a day.

It is impossible to imagine what the aqua vitae of ancient Ireland tasted like. Doubtless, the quality of the grains was high, but they had no idea what yeast was; perhaps the early distillers saved some yeast from the foam of the mash, an early stage of the whiskey-making process, or else they relied on wild, airborne yeast. It is probable that the first distillers also consumed their whiskey soon after distillation. The idea of aging in wood no doubt came after years of experimentation.

Whiskey history is obscure, but we know two things for sure: it was a volatile and impure liquor, but it had (and has) medicinal qualities.

The value of aqua vitae as a benefit to human health was unquestioned. The quality of food and water throughout the world was always in question. Distillation, therefore, was a purification of matter, a transformation of the ordinary into spiritual state. A draught of the spirit could negate the impurities ingested into the body during the normal course of a meal. It was considered also to be a restorative remedy for sickness. We know this from our grandmothers, yet the government of this country seeks to quell all knowledge of this common and delightful cure.

The other certainty was this: the high concentration of impurities in homemade whiskey had the potential to impart a ferocious headache and a stupendous hangover. No wonder the Irish have a predilection for cabbage. That vegetable is one of the few on earth that contains a compound said to alleviate the discomfort encountered on the morning after an evening of insobriety.

St. Patrick's legacy influenced a nation steeped in Catholic tradition and study. So renowned was Ireland for its religious scholarship that it attracted priests and monks from all Christendom. In most of the European lands dotted with monasteries, the men who took holy orders also took to making beer, wine, and spirits. It was the Irish brothers, therefore, who slowly refined the art of distillation, thereby refining the whiskey itself.

Make no mistake: the Irish were the world's first distillers of spirits. This is not to denigrate anything Scottish; the Scotch whisky experience is as complex and rewarding as that of Irish whiskey. But be it known that the people of Ireland were distilling whiskey at a time when the Picts, the predecessors of the Scots (who came from Ireland in the first place), were still smearing their bodies with blue paint and stealing cattle in the Lowlands.

Much of the history of Ireland contains events unpleasant and disappointing to the Irish, which is yet another reason God gave them the whiskey—so that they could endure strife. It was one such unpleasantness that gave the outside world its first taste of the Water of Life. In the 1100s, King Henry II of England sent his soldiers west to invade Hibernia—the first of many unwelcome visits by the Crown. They burned and looted and inflicted the usual pain on the Irish people, but they also discovered that the locals enjoyed something they called uisge beatha. The British soldiers were not cunning linguists and could not properly mouth the Gaelic, so they bastardized the first word a few times and, eventually, it came to be pronounced "whiskey." They also discovered that they enjoyed drinking it and brought some home with them, to the delight of their countrymen, and even became promoters of this saintly liquor on their travels around the globe.

The rest of the history of Irish whiskey reads just like the history of the rest of the world: the efforts of the government to suck taxes out of the people. By the 1500s, the government in Ireland was English, and England was ever in search of sources of revenue with which to support its imperialistic expansion. Levying of punitive laws and fees on illicit stills and distillers, and even on raw materials used in making whiskey, increased over the next several centuries. The stills went underground, out into the bogs, ever farther from the eye and reach of the exciseman. It is safe to say that every village, and many a farmstead, had an operating still. The "poteen" was often wicked—clear spirit, unaged, impure, highly alcoholic, but satisfying to the rebellious Irish soul.

In 1608, in County Antrim in what is now Northern Ireland, the first legal distillery was born on the banks of the River Bush. The fact that it was called "Old Bushmills Distillery" gives ample indication that the making of whiskey had gone on for some time in the village of Bushmills. It is told that in 1276, Sir Robert Savage, the local landlord, fortified his troops with uisge beatha before they took to battle. The 1608 license was granted to Sir Thomas Phillips by King James I, and the whiskey soon became a favorite among the nobs of London society. Its popularity spread and, within the next two centuries, the whiskey made at Old Bushmills became a favourite in the Western Hemisphere to the extent that most of the distillery's product was exported.

Fire destroyed the Old Bushmills Distillery in 1885, gutting all but one building. The loss was devastating. But the world needs whiskey, and the entire complex was rebuilt and operating within three years. In 1897, the distillery announced a special issue for Queen

Victoria's Diamond Jubilee: ten thousand bottles of its Pure Old Malt whiskey.

Two other great Irish distilleries were established in Dublin, Ireland's capital, in the late eighteenth century: John Jameson & Son in 1780, and Sir John Power & Son in 1791. Jameson is now the best-selling Irish whiskey in the world. By the end of the 1800s, it is estimated that more than four hundred registered brands of Irish whiskey were available in the United States alone.

Meanwhile, the poitin men still operated in the back country, smuggling in raw materials and smuggling out their unlicensed whiskey. The uncountable little stills in the hills and bogs gave rise to an army of excisemen and, for more than a century, blood was shed on both sides over the unlicensed distillation of uisge beatha.

The quality of the whiskey two hundred years ago probably was not as high as it is today, because competition among distillers was causing them to push the product out into the marketplace. Good whiskey must be made slowly and with care, but the probable coarseness of the whiskey back then was considered by the growing anti-alcohol contingent to be a contributor to the social ills. A government act in 1823 succeeded in placing strict controls on the distillation process and, while this meant more regulation and higher tariffs, it also meant a slower distillation and a whiskey of higher quality.

Booming though it was, the nineteenth century saw the beginnings of a long period of difficulty for the distillers of Irish whiskey. This led to a dramatic decline in the twentieth century from which the whiskey's popularity had barely emerged. Though production remained high in the 1800s, several factors combined to start the slide. The continuous increase in duties on spirits was only one of them.

Another was competition from other intoxicating beverages. Rum was a force to contend with, both in England and in the Americas. Cognac and other brandies were making inroads, and wine was well established in Britain. A third factor was famine. Nothing drove the Irish people from their homeland the way the potato famines did. Couple that with the evictions from their native soil by the landlords and it is not surprising that in 1847, more than two hundred thousand Irish left the island. Within a few years annual emigration was more than a quarter million.

But the greatest of threats to pot-distilled Irish whiskey was homegrown, born in the mind of Aeneas Coffey of Dublin. For many years, Coffey had been an exciseman, rising eventually to become inspector general of excise. After he resigned from government service in 1824, he put his wits to work and invented what became known as the Coffey still. This remarkable invention allowed for continuous production of grain spirit that was just shy of pure alcohol. It remains nearly unchanged in design to this day.

The Coffey still incensed and disgusted the Irish whiskey distillers. The big companies rejected it as an adulteration. But across the water in Scotland and England, the continuous still found a home. Soon the production of grain whiskey began to flood the market of the empire, but what was most offensive to the pot-whiskey distillers was that the grain spirit was being blended with a small amount of pure Irish whiskey and sold, both abroad and at home, as the real thing. Elsewhere in the British Empire, blended Scotch whisky began its long rise in popularity, further dampening sales of the Irish product.

For more than half a century, the Irish distillers and their supporters fought against the blenders. Even doctors came out on the side of the pot distillers, railing in professional journals against health risks from consumption of "fermented liquor...made from damaged grain, rotten potatoes, refuse molasses, or other waste." The cause in favor of whiskey purity was joined also by some distillers of fine Scotch, who saw the blending craze diminish their business as well.

Though the traditional distillers never won the blending war, two laws were set down in the first part of the twentieth century that gave some benefit to the distillers and consumers of fine whiskey. The first was that, henceforth, Irish whiskey could be made only in Ireland, and Scotch whisky could be made only in Scotland. The second was that all whiskey, whether distilled in the old copper alembics or in the Coffey contraption, must mature for a minimum of three years in wood. The Coffey still people didn't like that much, for it set back their production three years, but the result was—and is—a much better whiskey.

The early years of the twentieth century brought Ireland its independence from England (1916), but not without great cost. The 1919 partitioning of Ireland into north and south gave rise to two years of civil war, followed by economic war; England and Ireland closed their markets to each other. That shut off sales of Irish whiskey to Canada, Australia, a great deal of Africa, India, New Zealand, parts of the Far East, and parts of the Caribbean. It is estimated that Irish whiskey sales in the British Empire amounted to 25 percent of the whole business. That nice slice of the economic pie went to Scotch whisky.

As if that wasn't enough, the silly government on the other side of the Atlantic shut off the legal trade in liquor for fourteen long years, something they called Prohibition, which turned out to have done more harm than good both in the U.S. and abroad. Bootleggers had a picnic, and went so far as to promote inferior products as "Irish whiskey," which damaged the reputation of the real thing. And when the Prohibition ended in 1934, the producers of Irish whiskey did not have enough product on hand to reenter the U.S. market at once. Whiskey takes a long time to mature. Stocks were low, and the Irish suffered again.

Irish whiskey languished, and the number of distilleries gradually shrunk to a handful. But lo, along comes a trade endeavour to stir sales. Between 1966 and 1972, the remaining five distilleries formed the Irish Distillers Group, aiming to revitalise the global market for the original Water of Life.

Since 1987, old distilleries have reopened and new distillers are being opened as I write. New blends and many more new and exciting products are coming from this great land—Ireland.

Today we are comfortable with blended whiskey, with the single malts, and with the assurance that we can buy and savour fine Irish whiskey, the best that Ireland has to offer. The Divine Distiller has done, and continues to do, his part in blessing us with Irish whiskey. The Irish, with their music and their stories and poetry, have conquered our hearts, and with their uisge beatha they have banished our thirst.

I hope the following pages of information will help you enjoy the spirits of Ireland.

Slainte!

IRISH
WHISKEY
A Little Bit of Information

Bushmills

The Old Bushmills Distillery in County Antrim, Ireland, is located in the heart of a lush barley-growing area and along the banks of St. Columb's Rill, a tributary of the River Bush.

The oldest licensed distillery in the world, the Old Bushmills Distillery was founded in 1608, but even before that date there was evidence of magic in the air; in 1276, Sir Robert Savage, ground landlord of Bushmills, fortified his troops before battle with "a mighty drop of aqua vitae."

The Old Bushmills Distillery has always used the agricultural riches surrounding it to produce a very special spirit—and today it is the birthplace of four distinctive whiskeys: Bushmills Premium Irish whiskey, Black Bush Special Irish whiskey, Bushmills 10-Year-Old Single Malt Irish whiskey, and Bushmills 16-Year-Old Rare Single Irish Malt whiskey, a single malt Irish whiskey finished in three different woods.

Like its production process, Bushmills' ingredients have stayed the same over the centuries. First there is barley, which is examined, graded, and cleansed to perfection as malt. The malt is then dried in a closed kiln kept separate from smoke; exposure of the barley to heat brings a special smoothness to the spirit.

After the malt has mellowed for several weeks, it is milled into grist. The grist is mixed with water from St.

Columb's Rill at various temperatures and yeast is added to the resulting mixture. Because the river flows over beds of basalt, the water imparts a unique sweet flavour to the distilled spirit.

All whiskeys produced at the Old Bushmills Distillery are distilled three times in authentic copper pot stills. The primary and secondary distillations remove impurities, while the third distillation helps create a smoother, cleaner spirit and ensures the quality of the whiskey.

Bushmills Premium Irish Whiskey

The original and best-known whiskey from the Old Bushmills Distillery is Bushmills Premium Irish whiskey. Malt whiskey reserved for Bushmills is aged seven years in oak casks specially selected to bring out the light, delicate characteristics of the whiskey. When mature, this malt whiskey is blended with a single Irish grain that has a light aroma and hint of sweetness. The result is golden in color, smooth in texture, and delicate in flavour.

Black Bush Special Irish Whiskey

Black Bush Special Irish whiskey is a rich, dark blend that is comprised of a high percentage of pure malt whiskey. Malt whiskey that becomes Black Bush is aged nine to eleven years in selected sherry-seasoned oak casks before being blended with a small portion of a special single grain whiskey to enhance the character of the malt.

The combination is then returned to the cask for "marrying." As the whiskeys mellow together, producing a uniquely rounded bouquet and rich amber hue, the distinctive taste of Black Bush is born.

Bushmills Single Malt Irish Whiskey—10 Years Old

Possessing a warm, sweet aroma and well-balanced flavour, Bushmills Malt is a delicate whiskey crafted from 100 percent malted barley.

The malt used to make Bushmills Malt is deliberately dried in closed kilns. This prevents the malt from absorbing the fire's smokiness (hence, no smoky flavours are imparted to the final distilled spirit), while still retaining the character of the malt.

Unlike its brethren Bushmills Irish whiskey and Black Bush, Bushmills Malt is a single whiskey that, after aging ten years, finds its full flavour, character, and dark, rich hue. A blender's skills are never needed to enhance Bushmills Malt; its flavour and character evolve naturally over time in the carefully selected American bourbon oak casks in which it is aged.

Bushmills Rare Single Irish Malt Whiskey
16 Years Old

Bushmills 16-Year-Old Malt is a single malt Irish

whiskey finished in three different woods for unparalleled taste quality.

Unlike any other Irish single malt whiskey, Bushmills 16-Year-Old Malt is finished in bourbon, sherry, and port woods. To the already clean, non-smoky taste of fine Bushmills Irish whiskey, the woods add elements of depth and flavour. The result is a rich, smooth old malt with a wonderful complexity of sweet, spicy, and woody flavours.

Connemara
Pot Still Peated Single Malt Irish Whiskey
The Connemara Pot Stilled Peated Single Malt is a unique product, being the only peated single malt on the market.

Its name, Connemara, hails from the famous Connemara region in the west of Ireland. A region of wild beauty, with majestic mountains, soft rain, mist, lakes, and pure water carried eastwards by the Atlantic winds.

The Connemara Pot Stilled Peated Single Malt captures the natural beauty of this majestic region of peated lands and mountains.

The mash of pure clear spring water and peated malted barley gives the Connemara its unique and distinctive flavours. The natural ingredients and traditional distilling methods are employed to create a whiskey which, after slowly maturing for long years in oak casks, is simply unique.

The secret of the Connemara's special peated taste is in the drying process where the newly germinated malted barley is dried over a peat fire with smoke rising through it to add a famed and distinctive peaty flavour and aroma.

Connemara Tasting Notes

Nose: Intense peatiness for an Irish whiskey yet less smoky than an Islay, with a heathery bouquet and inklings of honey.

Taste: The sweetness of honey and spices gradually gives way to a smooth rise in the peated malt flavour, a good balance is struck with neither being overpowering.

Finish: The honey diffuses in the mouth as the peat lingers on. There is a delicate taste of vanilla and a sense of the matured oak. Intricate and amazing.

Comment: Unique in being Ireland's only peated malt, this is a mature, top class peat whiskey with a bright future.

John Jameson

In the eighteenth century, Dublin was the Second City of the British Empire and the seventh largest city in the world. Irish whiskey had already acquired a reputation for greatness, but among Irish whiskeys, the Dublin whiskeys were particularly prized. During the latter half of the eighteenth century, many famous distilleries were founded in Ireland's capital.

Among them was John Jameson. In 1780, during the golden age of Irish whiskey, Jameson founded his distillery in Bow Street near to the heart of Dublin. He quickly acquired a reputation for making the finest Irish whiskey in the world, a position Jameson still has today.

Jameson 1780 12-Year-Old Irish whiskey is the direct descendant of the liqueur whiskey which confounded Monsieur Hennessy in the 1920s, and will confound experts as surely in the twenty-first century. Its reputation as a digestive is as solid today as it was then and, despite the Irishman's love for brandy, a well-matured whiskey like 1780 has as sure a place as any fine cognac at the end of a good dinner.

John Jameson first established his distillery in Bow Street, Dublin, in 1780. From the earliest days he committed himself to producing the finest whiskey possible. By the end of the nineteenth century, his products had established a reputation for top quality all over the world. This was partly due to his commitment to the traditional pot still method of distillation which continues to this day. The cheaper whiskeys from Scotland were blended with substantial quantities of column still whiskey which, although quicker to make than pot still whiskey, had little flavour of their own.

Jameson Irish whiskey is made from pure Irish water and choice native Irish barley. Part of the barley used is first malted but, unlike their cousins in Scotland who dry their malt over an open peat fire, which gives a smoky flavour to the final whiskey, the distillers at Jameson dry their malt in a closed kiln, so that the smoky flavour is deliberately absent.

The art of the distiller is to separate and retain exactly those elements of the alcohol family which, when mature, will make a perfect whiskey (or brandy), and to discard those elements which are undesirable and give a poor flavour. In John Jameson's opinion, only three separate distillations in a pot still will achieve this perfect balance of flavour congeners. Only Irish whiskeys are distilled more than twice. Thereafter, the whiskey must mature for twelve years in specially selected oak casks in dark, aromatic warehouses. During this time, strange, almost magical things happen to the spirit: some of the higher alcohols evaporate through the porous oak of the cask; oxygen enters through the porous oak; and some of the natural wood extractives, called lignins, are dissolved by the spirit. It is these lignins that give the whiskey its color. Only time will complete this slow interaction called maturation. There are no shortcuts in the making of a great whiskey.

Jameson is the world's largest selling Irish whiskey, and has been known worldwide for more than two hundred years.

Jameson is delicious when consumed on the rocks as in America, with water as in Ireland, or with soda as in England. It is also excellent in cocktails, because the absence of any smoky taste makes it uniquely mixable. Consumers today are finding the smooth taste of Jameson particularly agreeable.

Jameson 1780

One of the most charming stories ever told about Irish whiskey was by Maurice Healy, author of *The Old Munster Circuit*, in a book first published in 1940 called *Stay Me with Flagons*.

"Many years ago Monsieur Hennessy was visiting Cork and was entertained by the hospitable Dominic Daly, one of our leading citizens, and also one engaged in the wine and spirit trade. After lunch the host said: "Would you like a liqueur with your coffee?" Monsieur Hennessy concealed a grimace, and accepted. "Bring that peculiar decanter," said Dommy Daly to his butler. A few minutes later he turned to his guest and said, "Now, tell me what this is."

"Oh," said Monsieur Hennessy, "it is very difficult to be precise in these matters, but I should call it a Grande champagne...probably an 1893."

"It's a John Jameson Ten-Year-Old whiskey," replied Dommy.

Jameson 1780 should be drunk as a digestif, on its own, without water, ice, or soda. It should be served at room temperature in a glass that permits the nose to enjoy the aroma that rises from the spirit.

Kilbeggan Irish Whiskey

Kilbeggan Irish whiskey is an authentic product of Ireland.

It is distilled and bottled by Cooley Distillery Plc., in Riverstown, Dundalk, County Louth, and John Locke & Co., County Westmeath, the country's oldest licensed distillery dating back to 1757. Cooley Distillery is the only independent, Irish-owned distillery remaining in Ireland.

Kilbeggan is made from a mixture of locally grown grains including barley, corn, rye, wheat, and oats. Kilbeggan Irish whiskey is an excellent quality blend of aged grain and malt whiskeys.

While Irish whiskey is a first cousin to Scotch whisky, it doesn't have scotch's traditionally smoky taste. Kilbeggan, in fact, has a gentler, sweeter taste and a lighter finish.

The whiskey's exceptionally smooth taste is attributed in part to the lime-softened water from the nearby River Crann, which is used in making Kilbeggan.

"Kilbeggan" is Gaelic for "little church." What is now an idyllic village in the center of Ireland was, for many years, an active religious community built around a monastery. The first licensed whiskey distillery in the world was established in Kilbeggan in 1757.

Midleton Very Rare Irish Whiskey

Midleton Very Rare is the most exclusive and prestigious whiskey ever produced in Ireland.

Midleton Very Rare, like all Irish whiskeys, is distilled three times for maximum purity, from the finest Irish barley and clear pure water. Most other whiskeys are only distilled twice.

It is a blend of particularly fine distillates, matured in individually selected oak casks, in dark aromatic cellars for ten to fifteen years.

Each cask is monitored very carefully by the master distiller. When, in his opinion, the cask has reached the point of optimal maturation, the whiskey is drawn from the cask and included in that year's release.

Midleton Very Rare is a truly handcrafted whiskey of great complexity and subtlety of flavour, to be appreciated by the connoisseur of fine spirits.

Each bottle is numbered to record ownership and individually signed by the master distiller as a final guarantee of exclusivity and outstanding quality. It is then secured in a quality ramin wood gift case.

Paddy

Paddy is named for Paddy Flaherty, a salesman for the Cork Distillers Company in the 1920s. To meet the demand of distillery-bottled Irish whiskey, Cork Distillers sent out their best salesman, Paddy Flaherty, to make the new whiskey known throughout the area. He did so well that the customers began ordering "Paddy Flaherty's whiskey." Cork Distillers got the hint and the name "Paddy Flaherty" appeared on the bottle, later shortened to "Paddy."

Powers Irish Whiskey

In 1791, during the golden age of Irish whiskey, James Power founded his distillery in John's Lane near the Western Gate of Dublin. He quickly acquired a reputation for making one of the finest Irish whiskeys in the world, a position Powers still has today. When James Power died in 1817, he was succeeded by his son, who became Sir John Power and high sheriff of Dublin. John Power greatly extended the distillery and increased the popularity of Powers Irish whiskey at home and abroad. By 1891, the year of their first centenary, Powers was exporting extensively. They exhibited their produce at the World's Fair in Chicago in 1893 in the form of an enormous model of an Irish round tower made of bottles of Powers Irish whiskey.

In 1886, John Power & Son was one of the first distillers in the world to introduce the habit of distillery bottling. Before then, whiskey—and indeed wine and beer—was delivered in oak barrels and sold "from the wood." While in the oak barrel, these drinks continued to change and were liable to contamination. To protect the quality of their good name, Powers would mature the whiskey in their own warehouses under their own control and then bottle it for sale labeled with a distinctive gold label. Unlike wine, whiskey stops maturing when it is bottled, and customers started to call for "the Powers with the gold label" because they found that the quality was always reliable, always consistent. As a result, Powers became Ireland's largest selling brand of Irish whiskey, a position it still holds, and has been known around the world for two hundred years.

To achieve the maximum purity of the spirit, Powers, like all Irish whiskey, is distilled three times in huge copper pot stills. Finally, it is filled into oak barrels and put away to sleep for years in vast, dark aromatic warehouses. Only time can complete the magic of Powers Irish whiskey.

Tullamore Dew History

The origins of Tullamore Dew Irish whiskey can be traced back to 1829 when the Tullamore Distillery was founded in Tullamore, County Offaly, situated in the heart of Ireland. The owner was a famed distiller, Michael Molloy.

The location was well chosen—a rich agricultural and grain growing region, providing both the fine barley and pure water essential to the creation of good whiskey.

Following the death of Mr. Molloy, the distillery passed into the hands of the Daly family with Captain Bernard Daly in charge of the business. A keen sportsman, Captain Daly left the routine running of the distillery to one of his colleagues, Daniel E. Williams, who eventually became general manager of Tullamore.

Daniel E. Williams was the major influence on the expansion and development of the distillery, and his family became joint shareholders in Tullamore with Captain Daly.

His initials, DEW, inspired the whiskey to be named "Tullamore Dew" with its slogan "Give every man his Dew", which is still featured on every bottle today.

Not only was Tullamore famous for its Irish whiskey, but, in 1947 it also became the birthplace of Irish Mist liqueur, based on an ancient Irish recipe rediscovered by Daniel E. Williams' grandson, Desmond.

Tullamore Dew whiskey was used in the preparation of Irish Mist for many years.

For nearly fifty years, the whole Irish whiskey industry was badly affected by two international events that together caused a serious decline in the fortunes of all the leading brands.

The first event was the USA's Prohibition period (1919–1933), during which time a major export market disappeared completely. The second was a trade war with England in the 1930s which resulted in the loss of all Irish whiskey sales in England and the British Empire—including Canada, Australia, New Zealand, and parts of the Caribbean and Far East.

With the majority of Irish whiskey markets removed, the distilleries decreased their production and lowered their stockholdings of maturing whiskeys.

The final consequence of this chain of events was felt when Prohibition laws in the United States were eventually repealed. Immediately, demand was renewed—but the Irish whiskey industry had insufficient stocks to satisfy it (allowing Scotch whisky to gain a substantial position in the market).

Tullamore Dew, like many Irish whiskeys, was unable to sustain itself successfully through this difficult period. In 1965, the business was sold to Powers.

Between 1966 and 1972, all the remaining Irish distillers came together to regenerate the industry—ultimately under the name of "The Irish Distillers Group."

Production was also consolidated into two distilleries—Midleton Distillery in County Cork, where Tullamore Dew is distilled today and the Old Bushmills Distillery in County Antrim, Northern Ireland.

Tullamore Dew Production

Tullamore Dew is a premium Irish whiskey—distilled, matured, and vatted (blended) at the Midleton Distillery in County Cork, Ireland.

Its fine quality and distinctive taste are unique among Irish whiskeys. Connoisseurs describe Tullamore Dew's taste as "subtle, smooth, and with a pleasant maltiness combined with charred wood undertones and the natural flavour of golden barley."

Tullamore Dew is also considered to have "none of the overlaying smokiness of Scotch whisky nor the sweetness of the American bourbon."

This subtle, smooth flavour is derived from the unique way in which Irish whiskey is produced.

Natural Cereal Grains

One of the most important flavour components in Irish whiskey is unmalted barley, which is distilled with malted barley, in a pot still.

The malted barley is created by allowing barley to start growing in moist conditions, then stopping the growth by drying it over coal fires. This "malting" process brings out the sugars in the grain, which will later be turned into alcohol.

(The malting process itself differs from that used in Scotch. There, the grains are dried over peaty fires, giving

Scotch whiskeys their peaty smokiness. The absence of this is one of the defining characteristics of Irish whiskey.)

Mashing and Fermenting

The first stage in Irish whiskey production mixes hot Irish spring water with the crushed grains (a process known as mashing).

The resulting sugary liquid (wort) is collected and fermented by adding yeast to produce an alcoholic wash (with about 8.5 percent alcohol by volume).

Distilling

The wash is boiled in large copper pot stills and the vapor cooled and collected. This process is repeated to remove the harsh elements of the spirit and improve the quality of the final whiskey.

In addition, the Irish distill their whiskey in much larger pot stills than the Scots, providing further individuality.

It is important to recognize that the distinctive character of Irish whiskey is derived from the distilling, not the blending. This is why the Irish refer to distilling rather than blending, to emphasize that the skill lies in creating the distillates rather than blending them later.

Maturing

The distillates (the new spirits) are matured in oak casks that have previously been used for either sherry or bourbon production. They mature for a minimum of three years, although usually for much longer.

Vatting (Blending)

As with scotch, the flavorful pot still whiskey is blended with a lighter, more neutral grain spirit which serves to lighten the body of the final whiskey.

Blend variations are also achieved through the use of differing ages of whiskey and of different barrel types maturation, in casks previously used for sherry, rum, or bourbon, or in new oak casks.

The Tullamore Dew Blend

Tullamore Dew's particular taste character depends on the correct balance of mature whiskeys vatted together by the blender.

Pot still whiskey is the most important feature and provides the foundation flavour. Starting with a mash of both malted and unmalted barley, it is distilled three times in a giant copper still.

Grain whiskey has a simpler flavour than its pot still equivalent, being based on maize and a small proportion of malted barley. It is distilled in a continuous column still, again three times.

Tyrconnell Single Malt Irish Whiskey

The Tyrconnell is the flagship brand of one of the oldest distilleries in Ireland. A traditional single malt, it has a fresh malty bouquet, a smooth and subtle flavour, and a delicately dry finish.

The Tyrconnell Single Malt Irish whiskey is a premium Irish whiskey made from a mash of pure malted barley produced at a single distillery—hence, the description: single malt whiskey. In contrast, other whiskeys blend a variety of malt and grain products from several distilleries.

The Tyrconnell, an authentic product of Ireland, is from Ireland's only independent, Irish-owned distillery, Cooley Distillery, Plc., in Riverstown, Dundalk, which owns Andrew A. Watt & Co., of County Louth.

The whiskey is full-bodied with a fresh, malty bouquet, a smooth, sweet taste, and a delicate, dry finish.

The brand is named for "The Tyrconnell," a chestnut colt that raced to victory at one hundred to one odds to win the prestigious Queen Victoria Plate in the 1876 Irish National Produce Stakes. So impressed was the owner that he named his flagship brand of Irish whiskey after his beloved horse.

The Tyrconnell Single Malt Irish whiskey is available in 750 ml and 50 ml bottles.

A Bit o' the Others

Ballygeary
Launched in 1996 and available mainly in the United Kingdom. It is distilled at Cooley and blended by Invergordon, a Scottish distiller.

Buena Vista
The only blended Irish whiskey supplied on an exclusive basis by Irish distillers for the famous Buena Vista Cafe at Fisherman's Wharf in San Francisco, California. Used mainly for Irish coffee and sold only at the Buena Vista Cafe.

Dunphys
Was available in the U.S. until 1988, and is still available in the Irish Republic.

Hara
An Irish blend for the supermarket chain Intermarche in France.

Old Dublin
Available in retail stores throughout the United Kingdom.

THE REST
OF THE
BEST

Celtic Crossing

Celtic Crossing, a premium Irish spirit liqueur in the United States, came about as the result of a unique combination of heritage and creativity.

The delicate tasting liqueur is a blend of malt whiskeys, aged in oak barrels, with specially selected cognac from France. It is created in Ireland by the Gaelic Heritage Corporation, Limited, the product development and marketing arm of the Terra Group, an independent Irish company specializing in responding to niche opportunities in the world of international spirits.

Labels on the distinctive Celtic Crossing bottle and packaging refer to "150 Years of Irish Heritage," the number of years since the Great Irish Famine. A special product enclosure brochure ends with this toast: "To remember those who left Irish shores never again to see their homeland and to celebrate the heritage and achievements of Irish people around the world. Slainte."

Three different bottlings are offered. One is a signed and limited edition bottling ($80 suggested retail) in a ceramic crock based on the original three-legged skillet pot used in many Irish homesteads in famine times. It is packaged in a rope-handled box resembling a ship's lantern with the luxury crock positioned in a three-dimensional window. The standard bottling (750 ml, retailing for around $20) has six individual label facings visible through the honey-coloured liqueur. A trade miniature (50 ml) is also produced.

Cork Dry Gin

Cork Dry gin is a gin of distinctive character and great purity. On a base of the finest triple distilled grain spirit is laid down a complex blend of juniper, citrus fruit, and botanical flavours. On tasting, one is aware of these notes, but also of a background, almost a subliminally dry, slightly burnt flavour that is not found in other gins: this is the Watercourse* note, Cork Dry gin's unique ingredient that makes it that little bit different and very interesting.

Taste: Juniper with fruity citrus elements—orange peel noticeably. Also a vague medicine undertone, and "burnt coffee" taste. Very clean and well-balanced.

*Watercourse—a dry taste that is the trademark of Cork's historic Watercourse Distillery. No other gin has it. Cork Dry gin has 90 percent of the Irish gin market.

Irish Mist

The Story behind the Legendary Liqueur

A legend, it is said, is a story popularly regarded as historical. A story passed down from generation to generation. A story that has survived time. So it is with Irish

Mist liqueur, for it is time that has made Irish Mist truly legendary. Born over 1,200 years ago, Irish Mist has a heritage that parallels the heritage of Ireland itself. Here in this ancient land of rich, lush, green countrysides dotted with fabled castles and elegant estates, a most unique recipe was created. It was for heather wine, the very essence of what is today Irish Mist. At the heart of that drink, savored by the chieftains and nobles of Ireland's ancient clans, was a spirit touched with overtones of honey, herbs, and spices.

But when the clans left their beloved country for wars on the European Continent, the recipe went with them. Regrettably, it was soon to be lost. Yet later, after its long, lamented absence, Ireland's heather wine was rediscovered for all time. The Williamses, a renowned Irish distilling family desirous of rediscovering the ancient drink of their land for their distillery in Tullamore, met a traveler from Europe.

He arrived, quite fortuitously, with the long lost recipe that the distiller acquired and transformed into what is now the famous Irish Mist liqueur. Inherent in this transformation was a devotion to the authenticity and originality of Ireland's legendary liqueur. First there was the mélange of distinctive ingredients to consider. Not one, but four great distilled spirits form the liqueur's heart. Each spirit has its own character bred by its grains of origin, the inherent qualities of its wooden casks, even the time and geography of its maturation. Indeed, each spirit is also the result of distilling traditions with centuries of heritage. Once the spirits have mellowed and matured, a time-honored blending mastery brings them together, and they are married. The marriage then leads to a resting period during which the four spirits become one. After a perfect balance is achieved, the blend is ready to be commingled with exquisite honeys and herbs. From the heather and clover that cover Ireland's landscape, the finest honey is naturally produced for Irish Mist.

Finally, as many as a dozen different herbs, exotic and delicately aromatic, are gathered from far and wide to join in and complete the marriage that has become legendary. The ultimate achievement is the taste of Irish Mist, a taste as luxurious as the package in which the liqueur is presented. In tribute to Irish Mist's ancient heritage and Irish traditions, there's the elegant decanter-style bottle. Its jewel-like facets sparkle with a clarity reminiscent of Ireland's prestigious Waterford crystal, after which it was designed.

A classic, the bottle is enhanced by the sumptuousness of the Irish Mist label, a design inspired by the precious eighth century Tara Brooch, one of the finest works of Ireland's golden age. Equally treasured chalices as well as other rare brooches, shields, and regalia that adorned the royalty of the ancient clans provided further inspiration. Indeed, it is fitting that the treasures of Ireland embellish this classic liqueur.

The History of Mead

Mead is an extraordinary, legendary drink with strong attachments to Ireland. In fact, mead can be traced back many centuries before Christ. Up to the middle ages, mead was made from fermented honey and water by secretive monks. It was the chief drink of the Irish and was often referred to in Gaelic poetry. Its influence was so great that Tara, where the high kings of Ireland ruled, was called the House of the Mead Circle. Mead's fame as a refreshing drink spread quickly and soon a medieval banquet was not complete without it.

Even the church recognized the value of mead. Legend has it that St. Findian lived for six days a week on bread and water but on Sundays ate salmon and drank a full cup of mead. In addition, St. Bridget performed a miracle when mead could not be located for the King of Leinster—she blessed an empty vessel which miraculously became filled with mead.

Soon mead became very popular at weddings, where the bride and groom were toasted with the honey-based drink. On numerous occasions the groom, laced with generous amounts of mead, was carried by his friends to the bedside of his bride. If nine months later a bouncing baby boy appeared, credit was given to the mead and its maker.

The monks' secret method of making mead was lost during the tumultuous years of the Middle Ages. It wasn't until modern times that it reappeared. Today, mead is once again being produced by the Irish at Bunratty Meade & Liqueur Co. Ltd., Bunratty, County Clare, Ireland. The result is a drink fit for a king.

The Perfect Finale to Wedding Receptions: How Mead Became Wedded to Marriages

Have you ever attended a wedding reception where there seemed to be quite a bit of awkwardness and confusion at the end? What seems to happen quite often is that every aspect of the wedding and reception is carefully planned, according to custom and family tradition—except for the ending.

So the bride and groom usually go quietly off to change their clothes and slip away.

This certainly is not a new dilemma. As it happens, there's an ancient solution to the problem. How ancient? As far back as the Irish middle ages. The Irish had a tasteful answer to ending marriage ceremonies and celebrations: a toast with mead.

The ancient Irish drink of mead is once again bringing special meaning to weddings, and providing an excellent way to end them. After being lost for five hundred years, the recipe for mead has been rediscovered. So it is once again available to help properly send a bride and groom off with a final toast and special poem.

Today, many Irish weddings are ended with style and substance, because the full meaning of mead is one again understood. And the tradition is spreading as it did centuries ago.

Ever since the fame of the Irish monks' brew spread throughout medieval Ireland, it was believed that mead was essential for sending off the bride and groom after the wedding. Mead was used both as a final toast and as a proper beginning to the marriage. The bride and groom were provided with enough mead, and special goblets, so that they could toast each other for one full moon—hence the term "honeymoon."

This delicate yet potent drink was not only considered the best way to start a new marriage, it was also believed to enhance such valued qualities as fertility and virility.

The return of mead has revived the unifying tradition of a formal, final wedding toast to the bride and groom. It provides a focused finale to the reception and also revives the full meaning of "honeymoon."

Bunratty, the Irish distillers of mead today, have

created a special honeymoon gift, which contains a potpourri, a gift sachet for the bride, a bottle of mead, two glass goblets, and a special poem.

Bunratty Mead

Bunratty Mead is produced to the highest standards of quality and is based on a recipe that was a jealously guarded secret for over a thousand years.

Bunratty Winery, located in County Clare, Ireland, was originally an old coach house set in the shadow of the now famous fifteenth century Bunratty Castle.

Coachmen on their way to the west of Ireland would stop here and stable their horses for the night before continuing on their journey.

In 1979, the coach house was restored to house the original mead winery. It regularly receives visitors from throughout the world.

The distinctive flavour of Bunratty Mead is the result of taking the world's finest honey and carefully blending it together with selected herbs and wine.

In your own home, this superlative drink may be enjoyed both lightly chilled as an aperitif, or at room temperature as a table wine.

Poteen

The Original Irish Spirit for the Rest of the World to Savour

The illegal Irish drink is surrounded by myth, but one man has broken through the red tape.

It was truly a spiritual thing that the Irish did long ago when they trapped the purity and magic of nature to create from sunshine and rain, in the mountains and valleys, the original treasured spirit poteen of the Celtic isle of saints and scholars.

Over many centuries, the manufacture of poteen (so called because it was distilled in pot stills in remote areas throughout Ireland) has been praised in song and story.

Distilling poteen—or poitin if you like—has been illegal in Ireland since the Crown imposed a levy on spirits in 1661. Until now, that is. For in the pleasant village of Bunratty in County Clare under the shadow of its historic castle, Oliver Dillon is making the stuff with the full legal sanction of the Irish Revenue Commissioners, provided he doesn't sell it in his own country.

Oliver Dillon is the managing director of the Bunratty Meade & Liqueur Company, which has been producing mead for the past ten plus years.

For some years now Oliver Dillon has cherished the idea of making poteen and trying to win back its ancient good name, presently tarnished by tales of stills in pigsties and on mountain tops producing spirits from potatoes and beet. He said: "Poitin should only be made from the best of malt, barley, yeast, sugar, and water."

So his next step was to gain official approval. Years ago, he approached the commissioners, the Republic's equivalent of the customs and excise. Their first reaction was to say that they were not impressed. But Oliver Dillon persisted and, after two years, he received permission. "Poitin," which simply means "little pot," is the name Dillon prefers, as it is the Gaelic version. Poteen is the anglicized one.

Hackler
Poitin Irish Spirit
United Distillers, the spirits company of Guinness PLC, launched Hackler Irish Poitin on March 17, 1997. The product, which is distilled under license at Cooley Distillery near Dundalk, County Louth, is a pure, high quality Irish alcohol. It has been developed by United Distillers to capture a significant share of the global young adult market for mixable white spirits.

Hackler is a refined, smooth, and legal version of the infamous poteen, illegally distilled in Ireland for over three hundred years. Made from pure Irish water and grain, Hackler has a unique flavour and character. Its production has been approved by the Irish Revenue Commissioners.

Hackler Poitin is based on an old Irish poteen recipe and relies on distillation techniques that protect its purity and smoothness of character. Its single source of production and United Distillers' distilling skills and quality controls ensure the purity and consistency of the product.

The Hackler bottle is a contemporary, attractive design. The bottle carries the story of the "Hackler from Grousehall," explaining the source of the name Hackler, a master weaver and craftsman:

"The Hackler of Grousehall was a distiller of highest quality illicit poitin in nineteenth century Ireland. The master craftsman would doubtless be pleased that after so many years, this pure and smooth tasting Hackler Poitin is now legally available. Hackler now brings the spirit of Irish welcome and fun to people all around the world."

IRISH
CREAMS

Ashbourne Irish Cream

Imported by Marie Brizard Wines & Spirits, USA

Ashbourne Irish cream liqueur is a quality Irish cream liqueur which is produced in Waterford, Ireland, for the international wine and spirits company Marie Brizard.

The cream comes from one of the largest dairies in Ireland. This dairy is famous for its cream's quality and consistency. The marriage of this superb cream with Irish spirits is completed in an ultramodern plant near the village of Ashbourne, in Waterford. Both facilities are internationally recognized for their quality and process controls.

Baileys Irish Cream Liqueur

The success of Baileys Irish cream liqueur is more than just the luck of the Irish. It is the creation of a mixture with the richness of cream, the tastes of vanilla and chocolate, and the spirit of fine Irish whiskey.

Baileys is made from fresh dairy cream (not more than two hours old), Irish whiskey, and natural flavorings. The mixture is then homogenized to ensure uniformity in every bottle, pasteurized to preserve freshness, and then cooled and bottled. The Irish whiskey acts as a preservative of the cream, which is why Baileys does not have to be refrigerated, though it should be stored between forty to eighty degrees Fahrenheit.

Baileys was introduced in the U.S. in 1979 after five years of painstaking research in dairy product technology. It is the first liqueur to successfully create a blend of real cream and spirits that is shelf-stable. Baileys has spawned a slew of imitators, but none of them have succeeded in capturing America's imagination—and taste buds—as has Baileys Original Irish cream liqueur.

Most people consume Baileys straight up or on the rocks, though it is increasingly being used for a variety of mixed drinks. In winter it is often mixed with coffee or hot chocolate. Summertime consumption is moving to Baileys being blended with cream and crushed ice. Also, it is being blended with a scoop of ice cream into a cool, thick malt.

Baileys St. Patrick's Day 1998 Irish Cream Liqueur

Baileys Original Irish cream liqueur launched a commemorative 200 ml bottle specially designed for St. Patrick's Day in 1998. It was the first time Baileys had celebrated the Irish holiday with a special package.

The St. Patrick's Day limited-edition featured a distinctive green shrink-wrapped bottle with lucky shamrocks. The special St. Patrick's Day bottle retained the same bottle shape as the traditional Baileys packaging. The inspiration for the bottle shape was the style of the old Irish whiskey crock, the traditional jug used for storing Irish whiskey.

Carolans Irish Cream

Carolans Irish cream was developed in 1978 and launched in the United Kingdom in July 1979. Since the launch of Carolans, the brand has grown at a phenomenal rate to be the world's firmly established number two cream liqueur, marketed in over seventy countries worldwide with sales of over 500,000 cases.

Carolans Irish cream is named after the celebrated seventeenth-century harpist, Turlough O'Carolan. Blind from an early age, he became one of the greatest and most well-known traveling harpists in Ireland. His tunes were distinctive and many of his lyrics reflected his lively and cheerful character. Carolans Irish cream embodies the convivial spirit of its namesake. However, Turlough O'Carolan is not to be used for promoting the brand.

Carolans Irish cream is a unique tasting, high quality cream liqueur. The fact that cream liqueurs originated in Ireland is no coincidence, for Ireland has a great tradition in producing fine quality dairy products and distilling spirits.

It is the marrying of these two traditions and Irish expertise that lies behind the success story of Carolans. Carolans combines aged Irish spirits and rich double cream. It derives its superior taste from the subtle blending of flavours, principally honey. It is the touch of honey that gives Carolans its distinctively subtle flavour and differentiates it from other Irish creams.

This ingredient is very appropriate for a drink produced in Clonmel. The word "clonmel" is derived from the Gaelic "cluain meala" which means "vale of honey."

Clonmel, in County Tipperary, is also set in Ireland's famed "Golden Vale," probably the best natural dairyland in the world. Only the best suppliers are considered since the cream is such a vital component, making up over a third of the product. It is this uncompromising quality and use of the finest cream that gives Carolans such a smooth consistency.

Basically, there are four stages that go into the production of Carolans, combining traditional expertise with modern, highly sophisticated technology.

First Stage

Neutral spirit and Irish whiskey are carefully blended together in a vat at the plant to prepare the alcohol base for Carolans. Skill and experience play an important role in determining the perfect balance of spirits that are to be mixed with the cream. In addition, the alcohol base is closely monitored in the quality control laboratories to ensure exacting standards are met. When the right blend is achieved, it is mixed with the cream at a nearby dairy.

Second Stage

Cream, water, and stabilizers are mixed together at high temperatures in large stainless steel tanks at the dairy. Stabilizers are essential to make sure that the product does not curdle. Getting the mixture just right is a very delicate process and is tightly controlled using modern, sophisticated equipment.

Third Stage

After an appropriate period, the cream mixture is fed through stainless steel piping to a homogenizer. During this process, the spirits, honey, and flavours are fed into the mixture. The homogenization process ensures that the cream does not separate and binds all the ingredients together.

The technology which binds the cream and spirit in Carolans is unique and highly specialized, ensuring long life and a full, fresh taste.

Fourth Stage

Following homogenization, the mixture is cooled and bottled at the plant. Prior to bottling, samples are taken from every batch of Carolans for analysis and quality control. This close attention to quality ensures that the highest standards are maintained and only the best product is bottled.

The bottling hall at Clonmel was extended in 1988 in response to the continuing success of Carolans. It now has one of the most modern, efficient bottling plants.

The secret behind the product's stability lies in the homogenization process. This breaks up the fat content into tiny molecules which remain suspended in the liquid and bound to the other ingredients; thus the cream will not separate from the liquid.

The technological advantage in the manufacturing process gives Carolans the best stability and the longest shelf life of all Irish cream liqueurs. On average Carolans will last in excess of two years unopened and one year opened, although it is best drunk within six months of being opened. While not essential, it is recommended that the bottle be refrigerated once opened to keep it at its best.

Carolans is perishable and must be treated in the same way as fine wine. Carolans stock should be stored in a cool, dry place between five to twenty-seven degrees Celsius.

The above cannot be overstressed. Good rotation ensures that product is always fresh and, while Carolans is the most heat resistant Irish cream liqueur on the market, exposure to excessively hot conditions will affect the subtle flavour characteristics of the product.

Devonshire
Royal Cream Liqueur
Few companies have successfully developed products from "the grape to the grain," but that's what Henry Devonshire & Co. Ltd., Ireland's independent wine and spirit producer, has achieved in truly remarkable fashion with Devonshire Royal cream liqueur.

This flagship brand encompasses four national heritages and weaves them magically together into a uniquely smooth blend of Scotch whiskey, French brandy, and fresh Irish cream from a traditional English recipe.

Devonshire Royal peaches and cream liqueur—the subtle flavours of luscious sun-drenched peaches, the finest French brandy, and fresh Irish cream are blended together to form the perfect partnership.

O'Mara's Irish Country Cream
The Irish cream category is vibrant, active, and profitable, and it's expected to continue to grow and expand on its popularity.

O'Mara's Irish Country cream is an authentic product of Ireland and is the first Irish cream to incorporate fine wine in its unique blending process. The wine base opens up additional retail distribution opportunities and provides a distinctly smooth flavour without a hint of harsh aftertaste.

It is handcrafted in the heart of Ireland's dairy region by Pat O'Mara & Co. of Abbeyleix, Ireland, an independent Irish-owned liqueur company. The freshest, sweetest cream in all of Ireland is supplied for O'Mara's from a little dairy down the road.

O'Mara's Irish Country cream has a unique bottle shape with a distinguishing magenta ribbon necker and wax-like medallion pressed with the O'Mara family crest.

O'Mara's Irish Country cream is available in 750 ml bottles.

Saint Brendan's Superior
Irish Cream Liqueur

Saint Brendan's Superior is produced in the Northwest of Ireland—an area renowned for the quality of its dairies and distilleries. Nestled in the lush valley of Lough Foyle, the dairy selects only the finest ingredients to give Saint Brendan's Superior its distinctive creamy texture.

Using a complex but natural process, local dairy cream is blended with an aged Irish whiskey to produce this blend. Saint Brendan's Superior is free of artificial additives and is made with only natural ingredients.

BEER
STOUT
LAGER

Beamish

Quality and tradition run deep at Beamish. The business was founded on January 13, 1792, as The Cork Porter Brewery—a partnership among merchants William Beamish, William Crawford, and two associates. The characteristically rich, nutty-tasting Beamish stout is brewed today with a pedigree yeast that goes back almost two hundred years. Strict control of the all-natural ingredients, including exceptionally soft water from the outskirts of Cork City, gives Beamish the unique flavour and character that has made it the number two selling stout brand in Ireland. Even the company's original seventeenth-century building in Cranmer's Lane still forms part of the Beamish & Crawford brewery today, although the firm has adopted thoroughly modern brewing technology to assure an optimal product.

Guinness

The Guinness brand is the best-selling stout in the United States and around the world. Brewed at Dublin's St. James's Gate Brewery, Draught Guinness is sought after by beer drinkers who appreciate its rich black color, smooth creamy head, and complex, well-balanced flavours.

Guinness has a fabled past and is proudly recognized as the original "stout." In 1759, thirty-four-year-old Arthur Guinness took over a small brewery on the outskirts of

Dublin. After signing a nine-thousand-year lease at an annual rent of forty-five pounds, Guinness started brewing ales and a relatively new beer called porter, named because its characteristically dark color and rich flavour were popular with the porters of London's Covent Garden. Guinness' porter was so flavorful, yet smooth, that it set the standard for other brewers. By the 1820s, the adjective "stout" had been added to describe Guinness. Since that time, many brands have tried but failed to duplicate the special appeal of Guinness. Today, Guinness is a globally recognized symbol of the Emerald Isle and, at home, is a traditional element of the Irish culture.

Draught Guinness starts with crystal clear water from Ireland's Wicklow Mountains, which contains the perfect balance of minerals for brewing a fine stout. High-quality domestic Irish barley is malted and mashed, then mixed with handpicked hops, dark-roasted barley, and a special strain of the original yeast used by Arthur Guinness to create the immediately recognizable deep black color, rich creamy head, and enticing flavour that is Draught Guinness.

It is said that Draught Guinness is "first drunk with the eyes." To serve the perfect pint, the 50-liter (13.2-gallon) kegs of Guinness should be dispensed by a gas mixture of 75 percent nitrogen and 25 percent carbon dioxide at pressure between thirty and forty pounds per square inch to produce the famous rich creamy head. Dispensed through the unique Guinness faucet, Draught Guinness is ideally served at between 8.8 and 22.2 degrees Celsius.

Draught Guinness is an experience for all of the senses. It starts with the visual appeal of a perfectly built pint of Guinness, with its majestic thick head and mysteriously dark color. The aroma of a Guinness offers hints of the brew's complexity and balance. And the taste of Guinness proves why it is known and respected worldwide. The taste of Guinness is a rich mix of roasted barley, a slightly caramel flavour that is balanced by perfectly selected hops to create a drink that is at once both dry and refreshing. The aroma and rich creamy head of Guinness is best enjoyed in the classic tulip-shaped pint glass. Guinness is a great accompaniment to a wide range of fine foods. For example, try Guinness with oysters and shellfish or roast-ed meats and wild game.

While the Guinness brand is more than two centuries old, the popularity of Draught Guinness continues to increase. During the last ten years, this explosive growth has averaged 17.1 percent a year. By 2001, about two million pints of Guinness were sold within the year.

Guinness is perhaps the world's most literary-minded beer. George Bernard Shaw, Sean O'Casey, Brian

O'Nalan, James Joyce, and Graham Greene frequently mention the famous Irish stout in their works. "Ask them haven't they got a Guinness. I'd just fancy a Guinness."—Graham Greene's *Stamboul Train*.

Draught Guinness has just ten calories per fluid ounce. That is less than most domestic lagers and about the same as skim milk. Draught Guinness has approximately 4 percent alcohol by volume.

Pub Draught Guinness

A pint of Draught Guinness is one of the most sought-after beers on earth. In fact, Guinness is the best-selling stout in the United States and around the world. With the revolutionary Pub Draught Guinness can, beer drinkers can enjoy the rich black color, smooth creamy head, and complex, well-balanced flavours of Guinness—even if they cannot get to their local pub. The revolutionary Pub Draught Guinness can was invented by Guinness to simulate the draught experience and has won the brewery international awards, as well as the praise of thirsty customers.

Pub Draught Guinness was first sold in the United States in 1992.

The first packaged Guinness was sold in earthenware, handmade bottles. Later, Guinness was the first beer with "crown" sealed caps that are still used today.

While Guinness is brewed in forty-two countries around the globe, all Guinness sold in the United States is brewed at the original St. James Gate Brewery in Dublin.

Harp Lager

The brand Harp Lager is a classic European-style lager brewed by the master brewers at Harp Brewery, Dundalk, County Louth, Ireland. A rich and flavorful lager, Harp is recognized for its crisp, clean taste. Harp is a favorite of lager fans across Europe and throughout the United States.

Harp Lager traces its roots deep in the Guinness brewing tradition. As consumption of lager in Ireland and Britain increased dramatically, Arthur Guinness, Son & Company saw the potential for a high-quality lager. To meet this demand, they transformed the Great Northern Brewery in Dundalk, a stout and ale brewery, into the Harp Lager Brewery. The master brewers of Guinness created a rich golden lager, brewed in the continental style, and named it Harp, after the symbol on the Guinness trademark and of the Irish nation. Harp is exported to more than thirty countries around the world. Harp's distinctive, refreshing taste has earned seven gold medals against international competition in Belgium's famous Monde Selection beer tastings.

Water from the beautiful Cooley Mountains is combined with the finest ingredients available in Europe. Barley malt from Ireland, Seas, and Hallertau, hops from Germany and the Czech Republic, and a prized lager yeast from Bavaria give Harp Lager its distinctive, refreshing taste. Harp Lager has 5 percent alcohol by volume.

Harp Lager is available on draught in 13.2 gallon kegs, and twelve-ounce bottles packed four six packs to a case. To guarantee proper dispensing, draught Harp should be dispensed with carbon dioxide or a carbon dioxide and nitrogen blend, through clean lines and in beer-clean glassware. Like all lager, Harp should be stored and served at 4.4 to 5.5 degrees Celsius.

Harp Lager is a sparkling golden lager with a pleasing aroma. Harp is a classic European-style lager, instantly refreshing with a hoppiness that is balanced by wonderful malty tones. Harp is a rich, flavorful lager with true Irish ancestry. Harp has the versatility to accompany fine continental cuisine or more casual fare.

The traditional recipe for a Half and Half combines Draught Guinness and Harp Lager.

In the United States, Harp Lager has grown steadily in popularity. Harp Lager is the number one selling Irish lager.

Murphy's Irish Amber

In 1854, James J. Murphy and three of his brothers, Francis J., William J., and Jerome, bought the premises of the former Cork Foundling Hospital. Over the following two years, the existing buildings were adapted, where appropriate, and other construction added to form Lady's Well Brewery, which commenced operations in 1856 under the style of James J. Murphy & Co.

The Murphy brothers were members of a family that had, over the previous sixty years or so, established itself as one of the wealthiest and most successful in Cork city. The family had made the larger part of its fortune in tanning, tea-importing, and distilling.

When Lady's Well Brewery went into production, there were already three successful breweries in Cork: Beamish & Crawford, Lane & Co., and Sir John Arnott & Co. Many considered the Murphy brothers' new venture very foolhardy. A nineteenth century account asserts:

"Yet, undeterred by all the obstacles that beset their path, undaunted by the influences against which they had to combat, the Messrs. Murphy put their shoulders to the wheel and soon came to be recognized as one of the principal brewing establishments in our city."

The new firm established a reputation for its products and trade grew steadily through the latter decades of that century. By the late 1880s, it was producing more stout and porter than any of its rivals in the city. It was also acquiring a tied estate that guaranteed an outlet for its produce. New buildings and equipment were added as demand for James J. Murphy & Co.'s products grew. In 1892, a newspaper remarked that the extensive brewery premises "give an instructive insight into the prosperity that has attended the firm from its inception." Another account from 1894 states:

"It is difficult to describe with accuracy and fullness premises which are being almost daily improved, both as to construction and contents, and which are being constantly increased in size and importance."

The company had agents in a number of cities in Britain at this time and they enjoyed success in promoting Murphy's XX Stout, which was beginning to displace porter in popular taste. Efforts were also being made across the Atlantic. A contemporary source writes:

"In America, those of our exiled kith and kin in that country will be in a position to sip of the creamy stout brewed within sight and within sound of some of the most historic scenes of their boyhood's years."

In 1901, James J. Murphy & Co. took over the brewing firm of Sir John Arnott & Co. and, in the process, almost doubled the size of its estate of tied houses to nearly two hundred. The early years of the twentieth century were not unkind to the firm. It survived the first world war relatively well, but in the following years, the fortunes of James J. Murphy & Co. began to falter.

The Irish War of Independence and the Irish Civil War that followed caused severe difficulties between

1920 and 1923. The following forty years or so never saw the brewery regain the growth and success of its first fifty years. There was no real reinvestment and while the shareholders received their dividends, whether from trading profits or reserves, things drifted on from year to year.

In the 1950s and more especially in the 1960s, business was becoming very competitive, and tastes and lifestyles were changing. James J. Murphy & Co. did not at first react to these changes, but in the mid-1960s, it formed a joint venture with the Watney-Mann brewing concern of the UK to produce and market Red Barrel ale. New facilities were built and sales of Red Barrel quickly grew. Setup and distribution costs were very high, however, and placed a severe strain not only on the cash resources of James J. Murphy & Co., but also on the partnership with Watney-Mann. The partnership was dissolved in 1971, and the company was saved from liquidation by the state-owned business-rescue agency Taisci Stait (later Foir Teo).

In 1974, a large group of publicans formed the Licensed Vintners Co-Operative Society and bought 49 percent of James J. Murphy & Co., creating Murphy's Brewery Ltd. Two years later, they bought the remaining 51 percent from Foir Teo. During the second half of the 1970s, the range of products offered expanded greatly. Publicans were offered a wide portfolio of wines, spirits, soft drinks, ales, and lager in addition to stout. To fund expansion, the tied houses that for so long had largely sustained the brewery were sold off. A new bottling plant was built.

In 1978, Murphy's Brewery Ltd. launched Heineken lager in Ireland. While a number of disasters struck the company around this time, the Heineken connection was eventually to ensure the survival of the brewery. The new bottling plant was not a success. Youngers Ale, which had also been recently launched, failed. Market and other conditions adversely affected the brewery. Over the following few years, the crisis deepened and, in July 1982, a receiver was appointed.

Following protracted negotiations, Heineken acquired the assets of Murphy's Brewery Ltd. in 1983, and Murphy Brewery Ireland Ltd. came into being. This ushered in the latest and probably most successful period in the 140-year history of Lady's Well Brewery.

IRISH
COCKTAILS

A.I.

2/3 Cork dry gin
1/3 Grand Marnier
dash lemon juice
dash grenadine
lemon twist

Shake with ice. Serve over ice with a lemon twist.

ALASKA

3/4 Cork dry gin
1/4 yellow Chartreuse

Shake with ice and serve.

A TINKER TALL

1 1/4 oz. Irish Mist
3 oz. ginger ale
3 oz. club soda

Serve with lots of ice in a tall glass.

A-BOMB

1/2 oz. Baileys Irish cream

1/2 oz. Kahlúa
1/2 oz. Stolichnaya
1/4 oz. Tia Maria

Fill a shaker can halfway with ice. Put recipe into the can. Shake and strain.

ABSOLUT QUAALUDE

1 oz. Baileys Irish cream
1 oz. Frangelico
1 oz. Absolut

Fill a shaker can halfway with ice. Put recipe into the can. Stir and strain into sour glass filled with ice.

AFTER 8

1/2 oz. Baileys Irish cream
1/2 oz. Kahlúa
1/2 oz. green crème de menthe

Shake. Serve straight up in a shot glass.

ALMOND COW

1 1/2 oz. O'Mara's Irish country cream
1/2 oz. Lazzaroni amaretto
2 oz. half & half

Shake together well; pour over ice.

AMBUSH

1 oz. Bushmills Irish whiskey
1 oz. amaretto
5 oz. coffee

Serve hot in a mug. Top with whipped cream if desired.

AUNT ROSE

1 1/4 oz. Irish Mist
2 oz. cranberry juice
2 oz. orange juice

Shake. Serve in a tall glass with ice.

B ORIGINAL

The traditional way to enjoy Baileys is to serve a double measure in its own special glass at room temperature. In warmer weather many prefer it chilled before serving.

B-52

1 part Baileys Irish cream
1 part Kahlúa
1 part triple sec

Layer into a small snifter or large shot glass.

BAILEY SHILLELAGH

1 part Baileys Irish cream
1 part Romana sambuca

BAILEYS & COFFEE

Pour 1 1/2 oz. Baileys Irish cream into a cup of steaming coffee.

BAILEYS ALEXANDER

2 oz. Baileys Irish cream
1 part cognac

Shake well with ice and serve on the rocks or strain into a cocktail glass.

BAILEYS ALMOND CREAM

2 parts Baileys Irish cream
2 parts light cream
dash pure almond extract

Combine all ingredients in shaker. Shake and pour over ice.

BAILEYS CHOCOLATE
COVERED CHERRY

1/2 oz. Baileys Irish cream
1/2 oz. grenadine
1/2 oz. Kahlúa

*Layer grenadine, Kahlúa, and then Baileys. Serve as a shot
or on the rocks.*

BAILEYS COCONUT FRAPPE

2 parts Baileys Irish cream
1 part Malibu rum
2 parts milk

*Shake or blend until frothy; pour over ice and garnish with
toasted coconut.*

BAILEYS CREAM DREAM

2 oz. Baileys Irish cream
2 oz. half & half
4 oz. ice cubes

Blend for 30 seconds.

BAILEYS CUDDLER

1 1/2 oz. Baileys Irish cream
1 1/2 oz. Disaronno amaretto

Combine ingredients for a truly spirited pleasure.

BAILEYS EGGNOG

1 oz. Baileys Irish cream
1/2 oz. Irish whiskey
1 medium egg
2 cups milk
nutmeg

Mix with cracked ice in a shaker. Strain and serve in tall glasses. Sprinkle with nutmeg.

BAILEYS FIZZ

2 oz. Baileys Irish cream
1 oz. club soda

Pour over crushed ice.

BAILEYS FLOAT

2 oz. Baileys Irish cream
2 scoops softened ice cream

Blend ingredients until frothy. Top with one more scoop of ice cream.

BAILEYS FRENCH DREAM

1 1/2 oz. Baileys Irish cream
1/2 oz. raspberry liqueur
2 oz. half & half
4 oz. ice cubes

Blend for 30 seconds.

BAILEYS GODET TRUFFLE

1 part Baileys Irish cream
1 part Godet

Serve on the rocks.

BAILEYS HOT MILK PUNCH

1 oz. Baileys Irish cream
1/4 oz. cognac
1 1/2 tsp. sugar
3 parts hot milk
dash freshly ground nutmeg

Combine Baileys and cognac to dissolve sugar. Add hot milk and stir. Sprinkle with nutmeg.

BAILEYS ICED CAPPUCCINO

1/2 cup ice
2 oz. Baileys Irish cream
5 oz. double-strength coffee
1 oz. half & half
2 tsp. sugar

Brew a pot of double-strength coffee and set aside to cool. In a blender combine ingredients. Blend for 10 seconds and pour into a 10 oz. glass filled with ice. Top with a dollop of whipped cream and a sprinkle of cinnamon if desired.

BAILEYS IRISH COFFEE

1 part Baileys Irish cream
1/2 part Irish whiskey
4 parts freshly brewed coffee
1 tbsp. whipped sweetened cream

After brewing coffee, combine with Baileys and whiskey. Top with cream.

BAILEYS ITALIAN DREAM

1 1/2 oz. Baileys Irish cream
1/2 oz. Disaronno amaretto
2 oz. half & half
4 oz. ice cubes

Blend for 30 seconds and serve.

BAILEYS MINT KISS

2 parts Baileys Irish cream
5 parts coffee
1 part Rumple Minze peppermint schnapps

Top with fresh whipped cream.

BAILEYS MIST

2 oz. Baileys Irish cream

Pour in a glass filled with crushed ice.

BAILEYS O'

1 part Baileys Irish cream
1 part Stolichnaya Ohranj

BAILEYS ROMA

1 part Baileys Irish cream
1 part Romana sambuca

Pour over ice and serve.

BAILEYS RUM YUM

1 oz. Baileys Irish cream
1 oz. Malibu rum
1 oz. cream or milk

Blend with ice.

BAILEYS SLIPPERY ELF

1 part Baileys Irish cream
1 part Smirnoff vodka

Serve in a shot glass.

BAILEYS SUNSET

1 part Baileys Irish cream
1 part triple sec
1 part Kahlúa

Gently layer the Kahlúa, then the Baileys, followed by the triple sec. Garnish with an orange slice for a triple layer of delight.

BALLSBRIDGE BRACER

1 1/2 oz. Tullamore Dew
3/4 oz. Irish Mist
3 oz. orange juice
1 egg white (for two drinks)

Mix all ingredients with cracked ice in a shaker or blender. Strain into a chilled whiskey sour glass.

BALLYLICKEY BELT

1 1/2 oz. Jameson Irish whiskey
1/2 tsp. heather honey (or to taste)
club soda
lemon peel

Muddle heather honey with a little water or club soda until dissolved and pour in whiskey. Add several ice cubes and fill with club soda. Twist lemon peel over drink and drop into the glass.

BANANA DREAM

2/10 Cork dry gin
1/10 Cointreau
2/10 Bols crème de bananes
2/10 lemon cordial
3/10 fresh pouring cream
lemon
chocolate flakes

Shake.

BARNUMENTHE & BAILEYS

1 1/2 oz. Baileys Irish cream
1/2 oz. white crème de menthe

Serve in a rocks glass over cracked ice.

BERMUDIANA ROSE

2/5 Cork dry gin
1/5 apricot brandy
1/5 grenadine
1/5 lemon juice

Shake with ice.

BLACK AND TAN

1 1/2 oz. Tullamore Dew
1 oz. Jamaica dark rum
1/2 oz. lime juice
1/2 oz. orange juice
1/2 tsp. superfine sugar
6–8 ice cubes
4 oz. ginger ale, chilled

*Combine Irish whiskey, rum, lime and orange juice, sugar,
and 3 to 4 ice cubes in shaker and shake vigorously. Put
remaining ice in a 10 to 14 oz. glass. Strain mixture into the
glass and fill with ginger ale.*

BLACK MANHATTAN

1 1/2 oz. Old Bushmills Black Bush Irish whiskey
1/4 oz. sweet vermouth

*Fill a mixing glass with ice. Add Old Bushmills Black
Bush Irish whiskey and sweet vermouth. Stir; strain into a
chilled martini glass or rocks glass filled with ice. Garnish
with a cherry.*

BLACK VELVET

1 part Guinness stout
1 part champagne

Layer the champagne over the Guinness in a champagne flute.

BLACKTHORN

1 oz. Jameson Irish whiskey
1/4 oz. dry vermouth
dash anisette

Stir well with cubed ice. Strain into a cocktail glass or serve on the rocks. Garnish with a lemon twist.

BLACKTHORN #2

1 1/2 oz. Bushmills Irish whiskey
1/2 oz. Noilly Prat dry vermouth
dash anisette

Stir with ice. Serve in a cocktail glass.

BLARNEY COCKTAIL

1 1/2 oz. Jameson Irish whiskey
1 oz. Italian vermouth
2 dashes green crème de menthe

Shake well with ice. Strain into a cocktail glass. Serve with a green cherry.

BLARNEY STONE COCKTAIL

2 oz. Kilbeggan Irish whiskey
1/2 tsp. Pernod
1/2 tsp. triple sec
1/4 tsp. grenadine
dash Angostura bitters

Shake well with cracked ice and strain into a 3 oz. cocktail glass. Add a twist of orange peel and serve with an olive.

BLOODY MOLLY

1 1/2 oz. Jameson Irish whiskey
3 oz. tomato juice (seasoned to taste) or prepared Bloody Mary mix
dash lemon juice

Pour into a tall glass over ice and stir, garnishing with a celery heart.

BLOOMIN' APPLE

1 1/4 oz. Jameson Irish whiskey
2 oz. apple juice
dash Cointreau

Pour into a mixing glass. Add ice, stir, and garnish with an orange rind.

BLUE BLAZER

2 parts Tullamore Dew
1 part clear honey
1/2 part lemon juice
1–3 parts water
cinnamon sticks (garnish)

Pour all ingredients into a pan and heat very gently until the honey has dissolved. Place a teaspoon into a short tumbler and pour drink carefully into the glass (the spoon prevents the glass cracking). Serve with cinnamon sticks.

BLUE FOR YOU

3/10 Cork dry gin
2/10 blue curacao
2/10 Bols crème de bananes
2/10 Cinzano (dry)
2 tsp. cream
1/10 pineapple
orange peel, green cherry, pineapple leaves

BOILERMAKER

1 1/4 oz. Kilbeggan Irish whiskey
10 oz. beer

Serve whiskey in a shot glass with a glass of beer on the side as a chaser.

BOW STREET SPECIAL

1 1/2 oz. Irish whiskey
3/4 oz. triple sec
1 oz. lemon juice

Mix with cracked ice in a shaker or blender and strain into a chilled cocktail glass.

BRAIN

3/4 shot Carolans Irish cream
1/4 shot peach schnapps

Serve in a shot glass.

BRAIN HEMORRHAGE

3/4 shot Carolans Irish cream
1/4 shot peach schnapps
dash grenadine

Serve in a shot glass.

BRAINSTORM

1 3/4 oz. Irish whiskey
1/4 oz. dry vermouth
dash Benedictine

Stir all ingredients in a tumbler or jug and then strain into a cocktail glass. Garnish with a twist of orange peel.

BRENDAN'S BULLDOG

3 oz. Saint Brendan's Superior Irish cream
1 1/2 oz. coffee liqueur
splash cola

Mix and serve over ice.

BRENDAN'S CHOCOLATE CHERRY

1 oz. Saint Brendan's Superior Irish cream
1/2 oz. coffee liqueur
1/2 oz. grenadine

Mix and serve over ice.

BRENDAN'S COFFEE ROYALE

1/2 oz. Saint Brendan's Superior Irish cream
1/2 oz. Grand Marnier
1/2 oz. coffee liqueur

Fill with coffee. Top with whipped cream.

BRENDAN'S COOL FIZZ

3 oz. Saint Brendan's Superior Irish cream
3 oz. club soda

Serve with crushed ice.

BRENDAN'S SMOOTHIE

1/2 oz. Saint Brendan's Superior Irish cream
1/2 oz. coffee liqueur
1/2 oz. vodka
1 oz. milk or cream

BRONX

1/2 Cork dry gin
1/6 dry vermouth
1/6 sweet vermouth
1/6 fresh orange juice

Shake with ice.

BUCKING IRISH OR IRISH HIGHBALL

1 1/4 oz. Irish whiskey
5 oz. ginger ale

Combine in an ice cube-filled highball glass. Garnish with a lemon twist.

BUNGI JUMPER

1 1/4 oz. Irish Mist
4 oz. orange juice
1/2 oz. cream
splash amaretto

Mix all but amaretto. Float amaretto on top.

BUNRATTY PEG

1 1/2 oz. Tullamore Dew
3/4 oz. Irish Mist, amaretto, or Drambuie

*Stir with ice and strain into a chilled cocktail glass or with
ice cubes in an old-fashioned glass.*

BUSHMILLS COLLINS

1 oz. Bushmills Irish whiskey
4 oz. sweet & sour mix
1 oz. club soda

*Shake Bushmills and sweet & sour. Top with club soda.
Serve over ice.*

BUSHMILLS FUZZY VALENCIA

1 1/2 oz. Bushmills Irish whiskey
3/4 oz. amaretto
5 oz. orange juice

Serve in a tall glass over ice.

BUSHMILLS HOT IRISH TEA

1 1/2 oz. Bushmills Irish whiskey
4 oz. hot tea

Serve in a mug and stir well. Add a cinnamon stick.

BUSHMILLS O'THENTIC IRISH KISS

1 1/2 oz. Bushmills Irish whiskey
1 oz. peach schnapps
2 oz. orange juice
5 oz. ginger ale

Add ice and garnish with a wedge of lime.

BUSHMILLS SUMMER SOUR

1 1/4 oz. Bushmills
2 oz. orange juice
2 oz. sweet & sour mix

Shake and serve over rocks in a collins glass.

BUSHMILLS SURPRISE

1 oz. Bushmills
1/2 oz. triple sec
2 oz. lemon juice

Shake well with ice and strain into a cocktail glass.

BUSHMILLS TEA

1 1/2 oz. Bushmills Irish whiskey
6 oz. iced tea

Serve in a tall glass over ice. Garnish with a lemon twist.

BUSHMILLS TRIPLE TREAT

1 1/2 oz. Bushmills
3/4 oz. amaretto
5 oz. orange juice

Serve in a tall glass over ice.

BUTTERY FINGER

1/4 shot Irish cream
1/4 shot vodka
1/4 shot butterscotch schnapps
1/4 shot Kahlúa

Serve as a shot.

BUTTERY NIPPLE

1/3 shot Irish cream
1/3 shot vodka
1/3 shot butterscotch schnapps

Serve as a shot.

CAFE BRENDAN'S

1 1/2 oz. Saint Brendan's Superior Irish cream
1 1/2 oz. coffee liqueur

Shake with ice.

CAMERON'S KICK COCKTAIL

3/4 oz. Irish whiskey
3/4 oz. Scotch whiskey
juice of 1/4 lemon
2 dashes Angostura bitters

Shake well with cracked ice and strain into a 3 oz. cocktail glass.

CARIBBEAN CRUISE SHOOTER

2/3 shot Baileys Irish cream
2/3 shot Kahlúa
2/3 shot Coco Ribe

Serve in a pony or cordial glass.

CAROLARETTO

1 part Carolans Irish cream
1 part amaretto

Shake or stir on the rocks.

CELTIC BULL

1 1/2 oz. Jameson Irish whiskey
2 oz. Beef Consomme or Bouillon
2 oz. tomato juice
several dashes Worcestershire sauce
dash Tabasco sauce
freshly ground pepper

Mix all ingredients with cracked ice in a shaker or blender. Pour into a chilled old-fashioned glass.

CEMENT MIXER

3/4 shot Irish cream
1/4 shot lime juice

Pour directly into a glass. Let stand for 30 seconds and drink will coagulate. Serve in a shot glass.

CHIP SHOT

3/4 oz. Devonshire
3/4 oz. Tuaca
1 1/2 oz. coffee

Serve on the rocks or in a shot glass.

CLARIDGE

1/3 Cork dry gin
1/3 dry vermouth
1/6 Cointreau
1/6 apricot brandy

Mix over ice.

COCKTAIL NA MARA
(COCKTAIL OF THE SEA)

2 oz. Irish whiskey
2 oz. clam juice
4 oz. tomato juice
1/2 oz. lemon juice
several dashes Worcestershire sauce
dash Tabasco sauce
pinch white pepper

*Stir all ingredients well in a mixing glass with cracked ice
and pour into a chilled highball glass.*

COCOLOU

1 part Carolans Irish cream
1 part crème de cacao

Stir well on the rocks.

COFFEE ROYALE

1 part Saint Brendan's Superior Irish cream
1 part Grand Marnier or Cointreau
1 part coffee liqueur

Fill with hot coffee and whipped cream.

COMMANDO FIX

2 oz. Irish whiskey
1/4 oz. Cointreau
1/2 oz. lime juice
1–2 dashes raspberry liqueur

Fill a chilled whiskey sour glass with crushed ice. Add Irish whiskey, Cointreau, and lime juice and stir slowly. Dot surface of drink with raspberry liqueur.

CONNEMARA CLAMMER

2 oz. Irish whiskey
2 oz. clam juice
3 oz. V-8 juice
1 tsp. lime juice
several dashes Worcestershire sauce
1/2 tsp. horseradish
several pinches freshly ground black or white pepper

Mix all ingredients with cracked ice in a shaker or blender. Strain into a chilled double old-fashioned glass.

COOL MIST

1 part Irish Mist
1 part tonic water

Serve in a tall glass with crushed ice.

CORK COMFORT

1 1/2 oz. Jameson Irish whiskey
3/4 oz. sweet vermouth
several dashes Angostura bitters
several dashes Southern Comfort

Mix all ingredients with cracked ice in a shaker or blender.
Pour into a chilled old-fashioned glass.

COUNTY CLARE COOLER

3 oz. Bunratty Meade
7-Up
ice
lemon slice

Serve over ice in a tall glass.

COWCATCHER

1 part O'Mara's Irish country cream
1 part Sarti sambuca

Mix together. Pour over ice and serve.

CREAM WHISKEY

1 part Carolans Irish cream
2 part rye whiskey

Stir well on the rocks.

CREAMED SHERRY

2 parts Carolans Irish cream
1 part Duff Gordon cream sherry

Stir well on the rocks.

CROCODILE BITE

1 1/4 oz. Jameson Irish whiskey
2 oz. orange juice
1 oz. Grand Marnier
1 bottle 7-Up

Serve in a tall glass with ice. Garnish with a slice of orange or lemon.

CUPID'S BOW

1/4 Cork dry gin
1/4 Forbidden Fruit liqueur
1/4 aurum (or curacao)
1/4 passion fruit juice

Shake with ice.

DANCING LEPRECHAUN

1 1/2 oz. Jameson Irish whiskey
1 1/2 oz. lemon juice
club soda
ginger ale

Combine the whiskey and the juice; shake with ice. Strain and add ice. Fill the glass with equal parts soda and ginger ale; stir gently. Add a twist of lemon.

DERRY DELIGHT

2 oz. O'Mara's Irish country cream
2 oz. half & half

Shake together well; pour over ice cubes.

DERRY DELIGHT (WITH A KICK)

1 1/2 oz. O'Mara's Irish country cream
1/2 oz. Copa de Oro coffee liqueur
1/2 oz. Burnett's vodka
2 oz. half & half

Shake together well; pour over ice cubes.

DINGLE DRAM

1 1/2 oz. Tullamore Dew
1/2 oz. Irish Mist
coffee soda
dash crème de cacao
whipped cream

Pour Irish whiskey and Irish Mist into a chilled highball glass along with several ice cubes. Fill with coffee soda. Stir gently. Add a float of crème de cacao. Top with a dollop of whipped cream.

DIRTY GIRL SCOUT COOKIE

2/3 shot Carolans Irish cream
1/3 shot green crème de menthe

Serve as a shot.

DOUBLE IRISH COFFEE

1 part Saint Brendan's Superior Irish cream
1 part Irish whiskey

Fill with hot coffee and whipped cream.

DUBLIN HANDSHAKE

1/2 oz. Baileys Irish cream
1/2 oz. Irish whiskey
3/4 oz. sloe gin

Shake with crushed ice. Strain into a cocktail glass.

ECLIPSE

1 1/2 oz. Old Bushmills Black Bush Irish whiskey
seltzer

Fill a highball glass with ice. Add whiskey. Stir. Top with seltzer. Garnish with a slice of orange.

EMERALD ISLE

3/4 shot Tullamore Dew
3/4 shot green crème de menthe
2 scoops vanilla ice cream
soda water

Blend first 3 ingredients and then add soda water. Stir after adding soda water.

ERIE TOUR

1/3 Irish Mist
1/3 Carolans Irish cream
1/3 Irish whiskey

Serve over ice.

ERIN GO BURRR

3 oz. Carolans Irish cream, well chilled

Serve chilled Carolans straight up in a chilled cocktail glass.

EXTRA NUTTY IRISHMAN

1 part Irish Mist
1 part Frangelico
1 part Carolans Irish cream

Shake. Top with whipped cream. Serve in a goblet glass.

EYES R SMILIN

1 oz. Baileys Irish cream
1 oz. vodka
1/2 oz. gin
1/2 oz. triple sec

Build over ice. Stir and serve.

FALLEN ANGEL

3/4 Cork dry gin
1/4 fresh lemon or lime juice
2 dashes crème de menthe
dash Angostura bitters

Shake with ice.

FIFTH AVENUE

1/2 oz. Baileys Irish cream
1/2 oz. apricot brandy
1/2 oz. white crème de cacao

Shake with ice. Strain into a cocktail glass.

FOUR-LEAF CLOVER

1 oz. Bushmills Irish whiskey
splash green crème de menthe
2 oz. orange juice
2 oz. sweet & sour mix

*Shake first 3 ingredients and strain into a cocktail glass.
Float green crème de menthe on top.*

FOURTH DEGREE

1/3 Cork dry gin
1/3 dry vermouth
1/3 sweet vermouth
2 dashes Pernod

Mix with ice.

FRUITY IRISHMAN

2 parts Carolans Irish cream
1 part Midori melon liqueur

Stir well on the rocks.

GEORGE BUSH

1 1/2 oz. Old Bushmills Irish whiskey
1 strip lemon peel
3–4 oz. ginger ale, chilled

Fill glass with crushed ice to 3/4 level. Add Irish whiskey.
Twist a lemon peel over the drink to release oil and drop it in.
Top with ginger ale.

GIMLET

2/3 Cork dry gin
1/3 lime juice cordial

Mix with ice.

GIN FIZZ

1 part Cork dry gin
juice of 1 lemon
1 tsp. of castor sugar

Shake and strain. Top with soda water.

GINGER MIST

1 part Irish Mist
3 parts ginger ale

Serve in a tall glass with a wedge of lime.

GINOLANS

2 parts Carolans Irish cream
1 part Gordon's gin

Stir well and serve on the rocks.

GLENBEIGH FIZZ

1 1/2 oz. Tullamore Dew
1 oz. medium sherry
1/2 oz. crème de noyaux
1/2 oz. lemon juice
club soda

*Pour all ingredients except club soda with several ice cubes in
a chilled highball glass and stir. Fill with club soda.*

GRAFTON STREET SOUR

1 1/2 oz. Irish whiskey
1/2 oz. triple sec
1 oz. lime juice
1/4 oz. raspberry liqueur

Mix all ingredients except raspberry liqueur with cracked ice in a shaker or blender. Strain into a chilled cocktail glass and top with raspberry liqueur.

GREEN DEVIL

2 oz. Tullamore Dew
2 oz. clam juice

Shake with ice and serve in a chilled whiskey sour glass.

GRIT COCKTAIL

1/2 jigger Tullamore Dew
1/2 jigger Italian vermouth

Shake and then strain into a cocktail glass.

GUARDS

2/3 Cork dry gin
1/3 sweet vermouth
3 dashes orange curacao

Mix with ice.

GYPSY'S KISS

1 part Irish Mist
1 part orange juice
1 part lemon juice or sour mix

Serve with a dash of grenadine (optional) in a cocktail glass.

HAVANA

1/4 Cork dry gin
1/2 apricot brandy
1/4 Swedish punch
dash lemon juice

Shake with ice and serve over ice.

HAWAIIAN

1/2 Cork dry gin
1/2 orange juice
dash orange curacao

Shake with ice and serve over ice.

HAWAIIAN HIGHBALL

3 oz. Tullamore Dew
2 tsp. pineapple juice
1 tsp. lemon juice
club soda

Combine the whiskey with the juices. Add ice and fill with soda. Stir gently.

HOT IRISH

1 1/4 oz. Tullamore Dew
1–2 tsp. sugar
1 slice fresh lemon
4 cloves
pinch cinnamon or cinnamon stick
3–4 oz. boiling water

Stud lemon slice with cloves. Put lemon slice, sugar, and cinnamon into stemmed glass. Add boiling water and Irish whiskey. Stir and serve.

HOT IRISH AND PORT

1 1/2 oz. Bushmills Irish whiskey
2 oz. port
2 oz. water

Pour into a saucepan. Heat to boiling point but do not boil. Pour into mug. Add a cinnamon stick and an orange slice.

HOT MIST

2 parts Irish Mist
1 part boiling water

Garnish with a slice of lemon and cloves. Serve in a goblet glass.

HOT TODDY

1 1/4 oz. Jameson premium imported whiskey
1/2 slice fresh lemon
4 cloves
2 tsp. brown sugar
pinch cinnamon
boiling water

Stud lemon slice with cloves. Put lemon, sugar, and cinnamon into a warm cup or glass. Add boiling water and whiskey. Stir well and serve.

ICY BRENDAN'S

3 oz. Saint Brendan's Superior Irish cream
2 scoops vanilla ice cream

Blend until frothy.

INNISFREE FIZZ

2 oz. Irish whiskey
1 oz. lemon juice
1 oz. curacao
1/2 oz. sugar syrup or to taste
club soda

Mix all ingredients except club soda with cracked ice in a shaker or blender. Strain into a chilled wine goblet and fill with club soda.

INSPIRATION

1/4 Cork dry gin
1/4 dry vermouth
1/4 Calvados
1/4 Grand Marnier

Mix. Add a cherry.

INTERNATIONAL COFFEE

1/2 oz. Devonshire
1/2 oz. Chambord
hot coffee

Serve in a mug.

INTERNATIONAL CREAM

1/2 shot Carolans Irish cream
1/2 shot Kahlúa
splash Grand Marnier
2 scoops vanilla ice cream
splash milk

Blend.

IRISH ANGEL

3/4 oz. Jameson Irish whiskey
1/4 oz. light crème de cacao
1/4 oz. white crème de menthe
1 1/2 oz. heavy cream

*Shake well with crushed ice. Strain into chilled cocktail glass
or serve on the rocks.*

IRISH APPLE

2 parts Carolans Irish cream
1 part Laird's Applejack

Stir well on the rocks.

IRISH CANADIAN

1/2 oz. Irish Mist
1 1/2 oz. Canadian whiskey

*In a mixing glass half-filled with ice cubes, combine both
ingredients. Stir well. Strain into a cocktail glass.*

IRISH CANDY

3 oz. Baileys Irish cream
1 1/4 oz. chocolate raspberry liqueur
1 oz. white crème de cacao

Build over ice. Stir and serve.

IRISH CELEBRATION

1 1/4 oz. Bushmills
1/4 oz. green crème de menthe
splash champagne

*Shake ingredients with ice and strain into a large wine glass;
top with champagne.*

IRISH CHARLIE

1/2 shot Carolans Irish cream
1/2 shot white crème de menthe

Shake with ice. Serve in a shot glass.

IRISH COKE

1 shot Baileys Irish cream
Cola

Fill with cola and garnish with a cherry. Serve in rocks or old-fashioned glass.

IRISH COLLINS

juice of a small lemon
1 spoonful powdered sugar
1 jigger Irish whiskey

Mix in a goblet with ice. Strain into a large, thin glass and fill with one bottle of soda. Stir with spoon.

IRISH COOLER

1 1/4 oz. Tullamore Dew
6 oz. club soda

Pour whiskey into a highball glass over ice. Top with soda and stir. Garnish with a lemon peel spiral.

IRISH COW

1 1/2 oz. Tullamore Dew
8 oz. hot milk
1 tsp. sugar

Pour the milk into a glass and add sugar and whiskey. Stir well.

IRISH COWBOY

1 part Baileys Irish cream
1 part bourbon

Shake or stir on the rocks.

IRISH CREAM STINGER

3 parts Carolans Irish cream
1 part white crème de menthe

Stir well on the rocks.

IRISH CRESTA

1 oz. Tullamore Dew
2 tsp. Irish Mist
2 tsp. orange juice
1 egg white

Combine with ice and shake well. Strain and add ice.

IRISH DELIGHT

1 1/2 oz. Bushmills Irish whiskey
3/4 oz. cream

Serve in a rocks glass with ice and stir.

IRISH DOWN UNDER

1 part Baileys Irish cream
1 part Stubbs Australian rum

Shake with ice and serve.

IRISH DREAM

1/2 oz. Carolans Irish cream
1/2 oz. hazelnut liqueur
1/2 oz. dark crème de cacao
1 scoop vanilla ice cream

Combine ingredients in a blender with ice. Blend thoroughly.
Pour into a collins or parfait glass. Serve with a straw.

IRISH EYES

1 oz. Kilbeggan Irish whiskey
1/4 oz. green crème de menthe
2 oz. heavy cream

Shake well with crushed ice. Strain into a chilled cocktail
glass. Garnish with a maraschino cherry.

IRISH EYES #2

1 1/2 oz. Saint Brendan's Superior Irish cream
1 1/2 oz. cream
splash cola
splash soda water

Serve long and tall over ice.

IRISH FIX #1

2 oz. Jameson Irish whiskey
2 tsp. Irish Mist
2 tsp. lemon juice
1 tsp. sugar

*Dissolve the sugar with a few drops of hot water in a glass. Add
whiskey and lemon juice; fill with crushed ice and stir well.
Add slices of orange and lemon and float the Irish Mist on top.*

IRISH FIX #2

2 oz. Tullamore Dew
1/2 oz. Irish Mist
1 oz. pineapple juice
1/2 oz. lemon juice
1/2 tsp. sugar syrup

*Fill mixing glass with ice. Add Irish whiskey, Irish Mist,
pineapple juice, lemon juice, and sugar syrup. Shake. Strain
into a rocks glass filled with ice. Garnish with a lemon slice.*

IRISH FIZZ

2 1/2 oz. Tullamore Dew
1 1/2 tsp. lemon juice
1 tsp. triple sec
1/2 tsp. sugar
club soda

Combine (except the soda) with ice and shake. Strain; add ice and club soda.

IRISH FLAG SHOOTER

1 oz. green crème de menthe
1 oz. Carolans Irish cream
1 oz. Grand Marnier

Pour ingredients in order given into a pousse cafe or cordial glass so that they form separate layers.

IRISH FROG

3/4 oz. Midori
3/4 oz. Baileys Irish cream, chilled

Layer in above order in a 1 1/2 oz. cordial glass.

IRISH FROST SHOOTER

1 shot Baileys Irish cream
splash Coco Lopez cream of coconut
splash half & half

Shake and strain. Garnish with cinnamon. Serve in a pony or cordial glass.

IRISH HEADLOCK

1/4 oz. Carolans Irish cream
1/4 oz. Irish whiskey
1/4 oz. amaretto
1/4 oz. brandy

Layer in above order.

IRISH HORSEMAN

3/4 oz. Jameson Irish whiskey
1/4 oz. triple sec
3 oz. sweet & sour mix
8 oz. crushed ice
1/4 oz. Chambord

Combine whiskey, triple sec, and sweet & sour mix with crushed ice. Shake well. Pour into a highball glass. Top with raspberry liqueur.

IRISH KILT

1 oz. Kilbeggan Irish whiskey
1 oz. scotch
1 oz. lemon juice
1 1/2 oz. sugar syrup or to taste
several dashes orange bitters

Mix all ingredients with cracked ice in a shaker or blender and strain into a chilled cocktail glass.

IRISH KISS

3/4 oz. Tullamore Dew
1/2 oz. peach schnapps
4 oz. ginger ale
2 oz. orange juice

Combine in an ice cube-filled collins or specialty glass. Garnish with a lime wheel.

IRISH KNIGHT

2 oz. Bushmills Irish whiskey
2 dashes Noilly Prat dry vermouth
2 dashes Benedictine

In an old-fashioned glass add a twist of orange peel.

IRISH LACED

1 shot Irish Mist
2 splashes Coco Lopez cream of coconut
2 splashes half & half
3 splashes pineapple juice
2 scoops ice

Blend. Garnish with an orange flag. Serve in a hurricane or poco glass.

IRISH MAGIC

1 oz. Jameson Irish whiskey
1/4 oz. white crème de cacao
5 oz. orange juice

Pour all ingredients over ice in a glass and stir.

IRISH MARTINI

1 oz. Bushmills
1 oz. Baileys Irish cream

Shake with ice and strain into a martini glass with dark chocolate shavings on top.

IRISH MIST ALEXANDER

1 oz. Irish Mist
1 oz. light cream
1 oz. dark crème de cacao

Shake ingredients with cracked ice. Strain into a cocktail glass. Sprinkle with nutmeg.

IRISH MIST COFFEE

1 part Irish Mist
1 part coffee

Pour into a coffee glass. Stir. Top with whipped cream. No sugar needed.

IRISH MIST KISS

Irish Mist
dash Hiram Walker blue curacao
splash soda

Fill a rocks glass with Irish Mist. Add blue curacao and soda. Serve with ice.

IRISH MIST SODA

1 part Irish Mist
3 parts club soda

Serve with ice and a wedge of lime or lemon in a tall glass.
Garnish with fruit.

IRISH MIST SOUR

2 parts Irish Mist
1 part lemon juice or sweet & sour mix

Shake well over ice. Serve in a tall glass. Garnish with fruit.

IRISH MIST STRAIGHT

1 1/2 oz. Irish Mist

Serve in a snifter or on the rocks.

IRISH NIGHT CAP

1 1/2 oz. Jameson Irish whiskey
4 oz. hot milk
1 tsp. sugar

Pour milk into a glass and add sugar and whiskey. Stir well.

IRISH PENANCE

1 part Carolans Irish cream
1 part Cointreau

Shake slowly and serve on the rocks.

IRISH POT OF GOLD

1 oz. Devonshire
1/2 oz. Goldschlager

Serve over ice.

IRISH PRINCE

1 1/4 oz. Jameson Irish whiskey
3 oz. tonic water

In an old-fashioned glass add ice cubes and stir gently. Drop in a lemon peel.

IRISH QUAALUDE

1/2 oz. Baileys Irish cream
1/2 oz. Absolut
1/2 oz. Frangelico
1/2 oz. white crème de cacao

Put recipe into a shaker can filled halfway with ice. Shake and strain.

IRISH RAINBOW

1 1/2 oz. Irish whiskey
several dashes Pernod
several dashes curacao
several dashes maraschino liqueur
several dashes Angostura bitters
orange peel

Mix all ingredients except orange peel with cracked ice in a shaker or blender. Pour into a chilled old-fashioned glass. Twist an orange peel over drink and drop in.

IRISH RASPBERRY

1 oz. Devonshire Irish cream
1/2 oz. Chambord

Blend with 1 cup of ice.

IRISH RICKEY

1 1/2 oz. Tullamore Dew
1 cube ice
juice of 1/2 lime

Fill an 8 oz. highball glass with carbonated water and stir. Leave the lime in the glass.

IRISH ROSE

1 jigger Irish whiskey
3–4 dashes grenadine
1 lump ice

Fill a glass from soda siphon.

IRISH RUSSIAN

1 part Carolans Irish cream
1 part vodka

Stir well on the rocks.

IRISH SHILLELAGH

1 1/2 oz. Jameson Irish whiskey
juice of 1/2 lemon
1 tsp. powdered sugar
1/2 oz. sloe gin
1/2 oz. rum
2 peach slices

Shake well with cracked ice and strain into a 5 oz. punch glass.
Decorate with fresh raspberries, strawberries, and a cherry.

IRISH SLING

1 jigger Tullamore Dew
1 jigger gin

Mix in an old-fashioned glass. Crush one lump of sugar and two lumps of ice and add to the glass.

IRISH SOUR

1 1/2 oz. Jameson Irish whiskey
juice of 1/2 lemon
1 tsp. sugar

Shake vigorously with ice until frothy. Stir into a sour glass; add a maraschino cherry and an orange slice.

IRISH SPRING

1 oz. Jameson Irish whiskey
1/2 oz. peach schnapps
1 oz. orange juice
1 oz. sweet & sour mix

Serve in a collins glass with ice and stir well. Garnish with an orange slice and cherry.

IRISH WHISKEY PUNCH

juice of lime
1 lump of ice

Add Irish whiskey to taste. Fill a glass with carbonated mineral water. Stir with a spoon.

IRISH WHISKEY SOUR

1 jigger Tullamore Dew
juice of lemon
1 barspoon sugar

Shake. Strain into a sour glass or serve on the rocks. Garnish with an orange slice and a cherry.

IRISH-CANADIAN SANGAREE

2 tsp. Irish Mist
1 1/4 oz. Canadian whiskey
1 tsp. orange juice
1 tsp. lemon juice

Combine and stir well. Add ice and dust with nutmeg.

J.J.'S SHAMROCK

1 oz. Irish whiskey
1/2 oz. white crème de cacao
1/2 oz. green crème de menthe
1 oz. milk

Mix in a shaker or blender with cracked ice and serve in a chilled cocktail glass.

JAGER SHAKE

1/5 shot Irish cream
1/5 shot Jagermeister
1/5 shot root beer schnapps
1/5 shot amaretto
1/5 shot cola

Shake with ice. Serve as a shot.

JAMESON JEWEL

2 parts Jameson premium imported whiskey
6 parts pineapple juice
4 parts peach schnapps
dash blue curacao

Shake with ice and serve over ice or straight up.

JAVA COW

1 part O'Mara's Irish country cream
1 part Copa de Oro coffee liqueur
1 part Burnett's vodka

Shake together well and pour over ice.

JELLYFISH

1/4 shot Carolans Irish cream
1/4 shot white crème de cacao
1/4 shot amaretto
1/4 shot grenadine

Pour first three ingredients directly into a glass. Pour grenadine in the center of the glass.

JOHN'S DELIGHT

3/5 Cork dry gin
1/5 orange juice
1/5 Cointreau
egg white
float fresh cream

Shake all ingredients and float cream.

KERRY COOLER

2 oz. Tullamore Dew
1 1/2 oz. sherry
1 1/4 tbsp. crème de almond
1 1/4 tbsp. lemon juice
club soda

Combine (except the soda) with ice and shake well. Strain and add ice and soda. Top with a lemon slice.

KINSALE COOLER

1 1/2 oz. Irish whiskey
1 oz. Irish Mist
1 oz. lemon juice
club soda
ginger ale
lemon peel

Mix Irish whiskey, Irish Mist, and lemon juice with cracked ice in a shaker or blender. Pour into a chilled collins glass. Fill with equal parts of club soda and ginger ale. Stir gently. Twist a lemon peel over drink and drop in.

KISS ME KATE

1 part Saint Brendan's Superior Irish cream
1 part crème de cacao
1/2 part raspberry liqueur

Serve as a shooter or over ice.

KOALA HUG

1 1/4 oz. Jameson Irish whiskey
2 oz. lemon juice
1 oz. Cointreau
dash Pernod

Shake with ice. Use a tall glass, ice cubes, a slice of orange or lemon, and straws.

KRAZY KANGAROO

1 1/4 oz. Jameson Irish whiskey
dash Pernod
2 oz. orange juice

Pour into a mixing glass. Add ice, stir, and garnish with an orange rind.

L'IL ORPHAN ANNIE

1 1/2 oz. Irish whiskey
1 oz. Baileys Irish cream
2 tbsp. chocolate Ovaltine powder (or 1 tbsp. chocolate syrup)
1 tsp. shaved chocolate

Combine all ingredients except shaved chocolate in shaker and shake vigorously. Strain into a chilled 4 oz. cocktail glass. Garnish with shaved chocolate.

LEPRECHAUN

2 oz. Tullamore Dew
3 oz. tonic water
3–4 ice cubes
twist of lemon peel

Put whiskey and tonic water in an old-fashioned glass, add ice cubes, and stir gently. Drop in the lemon peel. Serves one.

LEPRECHAUN'S CHOICE

1 1/4 oz. Baileys Irish cream
3/4 oz. Smirnoff vodka
club soda

Serve in a tall glass. Top with club soda.

LEPRECHAUN'S LIBATION

2 1/2 oz. Old Bushmills Irish whiskey
1 oz. green crème de menthe

Fill blender with 3 1/2 oz. cracked ice. Add green crème de menthe and Old Bushmills Irish whiskey. Blend. Pour into a goblet or large wineglass. (Courtesy of Beach Grill, Westminster, Colorado)

LIMP MOOSE

1/2 shot Carolans Irish cream
1/2 shot Canadian Club whiskey

Chill.

MAIDEN'S PRAYER

3/8 Cork dry gin
3/8 Cointreau
1/8 orange juice
1/8 lemon juice

Shake with ice.

MALIBU SLIDE

1 part Baileys Irish cream
1 part Kahlúa
1 part Malibu rum

Blend with ice.

MEADE SPRITZER

2 oz. Bunratty Meade
club soda
ice
lemon slice

Serve in a tall glass with ice.

MEXICAROLANS

1 part Carolans Irish cream
1 part tequila

Shake well with ice and serve on the rocks.

MILK & HONEY

1 part Irish Mist
1 part Carolans Irish cream

Serve in a rocks glass.

MINGLING OF THE CLANS

1 1/4 oz. Bushmills Irish whiskey
1/2 oz. scotch
2 tsp. lemon juice
3 dashes orange bitters

Add ingredients to a mixing glass with ice. Strain into a cocktail glass.

MIST OLD FASHIONED

1 1/4 oz. Irish Mist
orange slice
cherry bitters
sugar

Muddle orange slice, cherry bitters, and sugar. Add Irish Mist. Top with soda or water.

MISTER MURPHY

1 part Irish Mist
1 part white rum
1 part orange juice

Serve in a rocks glass with a dash of Angostura bitters.

MISTY MIST

1 1/4 oz. Irish Mist

Serve on shaved ice.

MISTY-EYED IRISHMAN

3/4 oz. Bushmills Irish whiskey
1 oz. peppermint schnapps
1 pkg. hot chocolate mix

Fill with hot coffee, stir well. Top with whipped cream. Optional: sprinkle with candy mint shavings.

MONKEY SEE–MONKEY DO

1 part Baileys Irish cream
1 part Rhum Barbancourt
1 part banana liqueur
1 part orange juice

Shake with ice and serve.

MS. TEA

1 1/4 oz. Irish Mist
3 oz. iced tea

Mix. Serve on the rocks.

MUDSLIDE

1 part Baileys Irish cream
1 part Kahlúa
1 part vodka

Mix and pour. Also delicious blended with ice and served as a frozen beverage.

MURPHY'S DREAM

1 part Irish Mist
1 part gin
1 part lemon juice
sugar

Shake. Serve straight up or on the rocks.

NEGRONI

1/3 Cork dry gin
1/3 sweet vermouth
1/3 Campari

Serve on the rocks. Add a half slice of orange and soda if desired. Mix.

NELLIE JANE

1 1/4 oz. Irish Mist
1/4 oz. Hiram Walker peach schnapps
3 oz. orange juice
1 oz. ginger ale

Mix all the ingredients and float the ginger ale.

NUT N' HOLLI

1/4 Irish Mist
1/4 amaretto
1/4 Carolans Irish cream
1/4 Frangelico

Shake. Serve straight up in a shot glass.

NUTTY IRISHMAN

1/2 shot Carolans Irish cream
1/2 shot Frangelico

Serve as a shot or on the rocks.

NUTTY PROFESSOR

1/3 shot Carolans Irish cream
1/3 shot Frangelico
1/3 shot Grand Marnier

Serve as a shot or on the rocks.

O'CASEY'S SCOTCH TERRIER

1 part Baileys Irish cream
1 part J&B scotch

Stir well on the rocks.

O.J. MIST

1 part Irish Mist
3 parts orange juice

Serve in a tall glass.

OATMEAL COOKIE

1 part Baileys Irish cream
1 part Goldschlager
1 part butterscotch schnapps

Serve as a shot.

OLD ETONIAN

1/2 part Cork dry gin
1/2 part Lillet
2 dashes orange bitters
2 dashes crème de noyaux

Mix with ice. Serve with an orange peel.

ORGASM

1/3 shot Irish cream
1/3 shot amaretto
1/3 shot Kahlúa

Serve as a shot.

ORIENTAL RUG

1/4 shot Carolans Irish cream
1/4 shot Frangelico
1/4 shot Jagermeister
1/4 shot Kahlúa
dash cola

Serve as a shot.

PADDY COCKTAIL

1 1/2 oz. Tullamore Dew
3/4 oz. sweet vermouth
several dashes Angostura bitters

*Mix all ingredients with cracked ice in a shaker or blender.
Serve in a chilled cocktail glass.*

PADDY COCKTAIL/IRISH
MANHATTAN

1 1/4 oz. Paddy Irish whiskey
1 1/4 oz. dry vermouth
dash Angostura bitters

Stir well with cracked ice and strain into a 3 oz. cocktail glass.

PADDY O'ROCCO

1 1/2 oz. Irish Mist
3 oz. orange juice
splash amaretto

Mix Irish Mist and orange juice. Top with a splash of amaretto.

PADDY'S WAGON

1 1/2 oz. Irish whiskey
1 1/2 oz. sweet vermouth
1–2 dashes Angostura bitters
1–2 dashes Southern Comfort
5–7 ice cubes

Combine all ingredients except 2 to 3 ice cubes in a shaker and shake vigorously. Place remaining ice in a chilled old-fashioned glass and strain drink into the glass.

PARKNASILLA PEG LEG

1 1/2 oz. Irish whiskey
1 oz. coconut syrup
3 oz. pineapple juice
1 tsp. lemon juice
club soda

Mix whiskey, coconut syrup, and fruit juices in a shaker or blender with cracked ice and pour into a chilled highball glass along with several ice cubes. Fill with club soda. Stir gently.

PATTY'S PRIDE I

1 oz. Irish whiskey
1/4 oz. peppermint schnapps
1 oz. club soda

Combine in an ice cube-filled old-fashioned glass.

PATTY'S PRIDE II

1 1/4 oz. Bushmills Irish whiskey
1/4 oz. peppermint schnapps

Serve on the rocks.

PAUL HEFFERNAN'S COCKTAIL JAMESON'S JEWEL

Ireland's entry to the International Cocktail Competition
2 oz. Jameson Irish whiskey
6 oz. Britvic pineapple juice
4 oz. peach schnapps

Top with 10 oz. lemon bitters and a dash of Bols blue curacao.

PEACH IRISH

1 1/2 oz. Irish whiskey
1 completely ripe peach, peeled, pitted, and sliced
1/2 cup fresh lime juice
1 oz. apricot brandy
1 tbsp. sugar, granulated, superfine (or to taste)
dash vanilla

Mix peach, lime juice, Irish whiskey, apricot brandy, sugar, and vanilla for 10 seconds in blender. Add 1 cup cracked ice and blend for an additional 15 seconds. Pour into a chilled 12-oz. glass, garnish with a twist and a slice of lime.

PICADILLY

2/3 Cork dry gin
1/3 dry vermouth
dash Pernod
dash grenadine

Mix with ice and serve.

POET'S PUNCH

1 oz. Irish Mist
1 cup milk
1 stick cinnamon
twist lemon
twist orange
1/2 tsp. vanilla

Heat milk, cinnamon stick, lemon, and orange twists to boiling point. Add vanilla and Irish Mist. Strain and sprinkle with nutmeg.

PRINCESS MARY

1/3 Cork dry gin
1/3 crème de cacao
1/3 fresh cream

Shake with ice and serve.

R.A.C.

1/2 Cork dry gin
1/4 dry vermouth
1 cherry and twist of orange
dash orange bitters
dash grenadine

Mix with ice and serve.

RED DEVIL

2 oz. Tullamore Dew
1 1/2 oz. clam juice
1 1/2 oz. tomato juice
1 tsp. lime juice
few drops Worcestershire sauce
pinch pepper

Combine with ice and shake gently. Strain straight up.

RING OF KERRY

1 1/2 oz. Tullamore Dew
1 oz. Baileys Irish cream
1/2 oz. Kahlúa or crème de cacao
1 tsp. shaved chocolate

Mix all ingredients, except shaved chocolate, with cracked ice in a shaker or blender. Strain into a chilled cocktail glass. Sprinkle with shaved chocolate.

ROAD KILL

1/3 shot Jameson Irish whiskey
1/3 shot Wild Turkey whiskey
1/3 shot 151-proof rum

Serve as a shot.

ROYAL ROMANCE

1/2 part Cork dry gin
1/4 part Grand Marnier
1/4 part dry passion fruit juice
dash sugar syrup

Shake with ice and serve.

ROYAL SMILE

2/3 part Cork dry gin
1/3 part Calvados
3 dashes sugar syrup
3 dashes lemon juice

Shake with ice and serve.

RUDDY MCDOWELL

1 1/2 oz. Irish whiskey
2 oz. tomato juice
dash Tabasco sauce
freshly ground pepper, to taste
6–8 ice cubes

Combine all ingredients (except 3 to 4 ice cubes) in shaker and shake vigorously. Place the remaining ice in a chilled old-fashioned glass and strain drink into the glass.

SAN FRANCISCO

1/3 Cork dry gin
1/3 dry vermouth
1/3 sweet vermouth
dash orange bitters
dash Angostura

Mix with ice. Add a cherry.

SAN JUAN IRISHMAN

1 part Baileys Irish cream
1 part Puerto Rican rum

Shake with ice and serve on the rocks.

SCHNAPPY SHILLELAGH

2 parts Carolans Irish cream
1 part peppermint schnapps

Stir well on the rocks.

SCOTCH IRISH

1 part Baileys Irish cream
1 part J&B scotch

Shake or stir on the rocks.

SCREAMING ORGASM

1/4 shot Irish cream
1/4 shot Kahlúa
1/4 shot vodka
1/4 shot amaretto

Serve as a shot.

SEMINOLE

3/10 Cork dry gin
2/10 Bols crème de bananes
2/10 Midori melon liqueur
2/10 pineapple juice
1/10 fresh cream

Shake. Garnish with orange or cherry.

SERPENT'S SMILE

3/4 oz. Jameson Irish whiskey
1 1/2 oz. sweet vermouth
3/4 oz. lemon juice
1 tbsp. Kummel
2 dashes Angostura bitters
5–7 ice cubes
1 strip lemon peel

Combine all ingredients (except 2 to 3 ice cubes and lemon peel) in a shaker and shake vigorously. Place remaining ice in a chilled old-fashioned glass and strain drink into the glass. Twist the lemon peel over the drink to release oil and drop it in.

SERPENT'S TOOTH

1 oz. Tullamore Dew
2 oz. sweet vermouth
1/2 oz. Kummel
1 oz. lemon juice
dash Angostura bitters

Stir well, strain into a small wineglass.

SHAMROCK COCKTAIL

1 1/2 oz. Bushmills Irish whiskey
1/2 oz. French vermouth
1 tsp. green crème de menthe

Stir well with cracked ice and strain into a 3 oz. cocktail glass. Serve with an olive.

SHAMROCK NO. 1

1 1/2 oz. Jameson Irish whiskey
3/4 oz. dry vermouth
1 tsp. green Chartreuse
1 tsp. green crème de menthe

Stir all ingredients with plenty of ice in a pitcher and strain into a chilled cocktail glass.

SHAMROCK NO. 2

1 1/2 oz. Bushmills Irish whiskey
1 1/2 oz. green crème de menthe
2 oz. heavy cream
maraschino cherry

Mix all ingredients with cracked ice in a shaker or blender. Pour into a chilled old-fashioned glass. Garnish with a maraschino cherry.

SHAMROCK NO. 3

1 1/2 oz. Bushmills Irish whiskey
3/4 oz. green crème de menthe
4 oz. vanilla ice cream

Mix all ingredients in a blender at high speed until smooth. Pour into a chilled wine goblet.

SHETLAND PONY

1 1/2 oz. scotch
3/4 oz. Irish Mist
dash orange bitters (optional)

Mix all ingredients with cracked ice in a mixing glass and strain into a chilled cocktail glass.

SIFI FLIP

1/2 Cork dry gin
1/4 Cointreau
1/4 grenadine
juice of 1/2 lemon
egg yolk

Shake with ice and strain.

SILVER SHAMROCK

2 parts Bunratty Meade
1 part vodka

Stir with ice.

SIXTY-NINTH (69TH) REGIMENT PUNCH

1/2 wineglass Irish whiskey
1/2 wineglass scotch whiskey
1 tsp. sugar
2–3 dashes lemon juice
2 wineglasses hot water

Use a hot whiskey glass. Imbibing the above adds greatly to one's comfort on a cold night.

SKIBBEREEN TONIC

2 oz. Irish whiskey
tonic water
lemon peel

Pour Irish whiskey into a chilled old-fashioned glass with several ice cubes. Fill with tonic water. Twist a lemon peel over the drink and drop in.

SLIPPERY NUT

1 1/2 oz. Saint Brendan's Superior Irish cream
2 oz. Roncoco rum liqueur

Serve over ice.

SOUTH WIND

3/10 Cork dry gin
3/10 peach schnapps
3/10 orange juice
1/10 cream

Shake with ice and serve. Garnish with an orange slice and a cherry.

SOUTHERN DELIGHT

1/4 Cork dry gin
1/4 Southern Comfort
1/4 Baileys Irish cream
1/4 pure orange juice
Mint leaves, cherries, lemon

Shake with ice. Garnish with mint leaves, cherry, and lemon.

SPEARAMISTY

1 oz. Irish Mist
1/4 oz. spearmint schnapps

Mix. Serve straight up or on the rocks.

ST. PATRICK'S DAY COCKTAIL

3/4 oz. Bushmills Irish whiskey
3/4 oz. green crème de menthe
3/4 oz. green Chartreuse
dash Angostura bitters

Stir well with cracked ice and strain into a 3 oz. cocktail glass.

SUNSET DREAM

1 1/2 oz. Cork dry gin
1/2 oz. crème de cacao
dash grenadine
pouring cream

Shake with ice. Top with whipped cream and a strawberry.

SWEET IRISH STORM

1 1/2 oz. Bushmills Irish whiskey
3/4 oz. Noilly Prat sweet French vermouth
several dashes Angostura bitters
several dashes Southern Comfort

Mix ingredients with cracked ice in a shaker or blender. Pour into a chilled old-fashioned glass.

TANGO

1/2 part Cork dry gin
1/4 part sweet vermouth
1/4 part dry vermouth
2 dashes orange curacao
dash orange juice

Shake with ice.

TARZAN O'REILLY

1 oz. Baileys Irish cream
1/2 oz. Smirnoff vodka
1/2 oz. crème de banana

Build in a shot glass over ice. Stir.

TERMINATOR

1/5 shot Irish cream
1/5 shot Kahlúa
1/5 shot sambuca
1/5 shot Grand Marnier
1/5 shot vodka

Layer.

THE BRANDYWINE

2 parts Bunratty Meade
1 part brandy

Stir with ice.

THE GREAT WHITE

1 1/4 oz. Jameson Irish whiskey
2 oz. apple juice
1 oz. white curacao

Pour into a tall glass with ice and garnish with a slice of apple or orange, a sprig of mint, and a straw.

THE HONEYMOONER

2 parts Bunratty Meade
1 part amaretto
1 part cream

Shake and pour over ice. Garnish with cinnamon.

THE ULTIMATE IRISH COFFEE

1 1/2 oz. Irish Mist
hot coffee

Serve in a warm mug. No sugar needed.

THE ULTIMATE TEA

1 1/2 oz. Irish Mist
hot tea
a bit of lemon

Serve in a warm mug. No sugar needed.

THREE-LEAF SHAMROCK SHAKER

1 oz. Bushmills Irish whiskey
1 oz. light rum
1 oz. brandy
1 tsp. lemon juice
sugar syrup to taste

Shake ingredients with cracked ice. Strain into a chilled glass.

TINKER'S TEA

1 1/2 oz. Baileys Irish cream
hot tea

Pour Baileys in a mug or cup. Fill with hot tea.

TIPPERARY

1 oz. Jameson Irish whiskey
1/2 oz. Noilly Prat sweet vermouth
1/4 oz. green Chartreuse

Combine with 4 to 5 ice cubes in a mixing glass and stir well.
Strain into a 3oz. cocktail glass and stir with cracked ice.

TO THE MOON

1/4 shot Irish cream
1/4 shot amaretto
1/4 Kahlúa
1/4 shot 151-proof rum

Serve as a shot.

TOASTED BRENDAN'S

1/2 oz. Saint Brendan's Superior Irish cream
1/2 oz. coffee liqueur
1/2 oz. amaretto

Fill with coffee. Top with whipped cream.

TOASTED IRISHMAN

1 part Irish Mist
1 part Kahlúa
1 part Disaronno amaretto

Shake with ice and serve on the rocks.

TOOTSIE ROLL

1/2 oz. Baileys Irish cream
1 oz. root beer schnapps

Topped with a dash of Baileys Irish cream.

U-Z

3/4 oz. Irish Mist
3/4 oz. Baileys Irish cream
3/4 oz. Kahlúa

Put recipe into a shaker can filled halfway with ice. Shake and strain.

VULCAN MIND PROBE

1/3 shot Carolans Irish cream
1/3 shot peppermint schnapps
1/3 shot 151-proof rum

Layer. Suck drink down through a large drinking straw in one gulp.

WHITE LADY

1/2 Cork dry gin
1/4 lemon juice
1/4 Cointreau
dash egg white

Shake with ice. Serve on the rocks.

WICKLOW COOLER

1 1/2 oz. Jameson Irish whiskey
1 oz. Jamaica dark rum
1/2 oz. lime juice
1 oz. orange juice
1 tsp. Falernum or Orgeat syrup
ginger ale

Mix all ingredients with cracked ice in a shaker or blender. Pour into a chilled collins glass. Fill with ginger ale.

WILD IRISH ROSE

1 1/2 oz. Tullamore Dew
1 1/2 tsp. grenadine
1/2 oz. lime juice
club soda

Fill a highball glass with ice. Add Irish whiskey, grenadine, and lime juice. Stir well. Fill with club soda.

WOLFHOUND

1 oz. Bushmills
3/4 oz. dark crème de cacao
1/2 oz. half & half
splash club soda

Shake with ice and top with club soda.

XIANTHA

1/3 part Cork dry gin
1/3 part yellow Chartreuse
1/3 part cherry brandy

Mix with ice.

YELLOW DAISY

2/5 part Cork dry gin
2/5 part dry vermouth
1/5 part Grand Marnier

Mix with ice.

THE STORY
OF IRISH
COFFEE

Ireland's Gift

Irish coffee, Ireland's gift to the list of great drinks of the world, is in fact a remarkably recent discovery.

Irish whiskey has been Ireland's national spirit drink for more than one thousand years, and the habit of putting whiskey into tea has been common ever since tea drinking became established in Ireland in the sixteenth century.

When transatlantic flying began again after the end of the second world war, the aircraft of the time—flying boats and the earlier Super Constellations—could not make the entire Atlantic crossing without having to make refueling stops. The most important of these refueling stops was at Shannon Airport, on the western fringe of Ireland and Europe, the last westbound stop before Gander in Newfoundland.

When these aircraft landed in Shannon Airport, the passengers had to disembark during the refueling and were often in need of a bit of refueling themselves. Joe Sheridan was the chief barman at that time in Shannon Airport. He took the traditional old Irish drink—whiskey in tea—and dressed it up into a new and more glamorous form to be attractive to the Americans, who represented the majority of the travelers at that time. He substituted coffee for tea, since coffee was more to the American taste, added sugar, stirred well to dissolve the sugar, and then topped it off with a layer of fresh, lightly whipped Irish cream. Finally came his magic touch of serving the drink in a stemmed glass rather than in a cup, since the visual appeal of the contrast between the black coffee and the white cream was instantly attractive to the guests. He never served it with a spoon or a straw but encouraged the drinker to drink the hot coffee and whiskey through the cool cream. Joe Sheridan found that he had only to serve three or four Irish coffees to the first few passengers to arrive in the airport bar, whereupon he would be immediately deluged with orders from the rest of them!

Because Shannon was truly a gateway between East and West, the fame of Irish coffee spread very quickly. In America it soon became a favourite drink, and one restaurant in San Francisco—the Buena Vista on Fisherman's Wharf—claims to have been the first to popularize Irish coffee in America: Stanton Delaplane, a columnist at the *San Francisco Chronicle,* brought the recipe for Irish coffee to his favorite watering hole and publicized Irish coffee unceasingly thereafter in his column. There is a bronze plaque fixed to the wall outside the Buena Vista's front door that records the fact that Irish coffee was first served there. To this day it is a sight to see the staff of the Buena Vista preparing more than two thousand Irish coffees every day! They are open 363 days of the year, closed only on Thanksgiving and Christmas Day.

The recipe spread to Europe almost as quickly. Within a very short time Irish coffee was being offered in all of Europe's top restaurants and bars, and it was established as a permanent favorite.

Today Irish coffee is as popular as ever. Many consumers have their first-ever taste of Irish whiskey in this way. They move on later to enjoy the unique flavour of Irish whiskey in its own right—with ice, with water, or with soda—the world's original and the world's greatest whiskey.

There is a bronze plaque also in Shannon Airport, erected by the grateful whiskey distillers of Ireland, to record the fact that Irish coffee was invented there by Joe Sheridan.

The recipe for Irish coffee hasn't changed since Joe Sheridan's day. The original is still the best:

Into a stemmed glass, put two teaspoonfuls of sugar, preferably brown; add one-third Irish whiskey and two-thirds really hot, really strong black coffee, preferably freshly brewed, not instant. The glass should be filled with this mixture to within half an inch (1 cm) of the brim. Stir well at this point to ensure all of the sugar is dissolved, and then carefully float over the back of a spoon a collar of lightly whipped cream, so that the cream floats on the top of the coffee and whiskey. Do not stir any more. Serve the drink without a spoon or a straw, as part of the pleasure comes from sipping the hot coffee and whiskey through the cool cream.

Slainte, agus saol agat! Health and long life to you!

TOASTS & WISDOMS

Health and long life to you,
Land without rent to you,
A child every year to you,
And may you die in Ireland.
—Old Irish toast

❖

To remember those who left
Irish shores never again to see
their homeland and to celebrate the
heritage and achievements of Irish
people around the world.
Slainte.

❖

Here's to health, peace, and prosperity;
May the flower of love never be
nipped by the frost of disappointment,
nor shadow of grief fall among a member
of this circle.
Here's to your health;
May God bring you luck
And may your journey be smooth and happy.
May you look back on the past with as much
pleasure as you look forward to the future.

❖

May the road rise to meet you,
May the wind be always at your back,
The sun shine warm upon your face,
The rain fall soft upon your fields,
And until we meet again
May God hold you in the hollow of His hand.
—*Traditional Irish Toast*

❖

Mother's Day
to a wonderful mother who always has
...a smile for our joys
...a tear for our sorrows
...a comfort for our failings
...a prayer for our problems.
Here's to Mother—on her day!

❖

Father's Day
To Dad:
from his children who acknowledge
their good fortune in being blessed
with a loving and dedicated father.

❖

To our host, an excellent man:
For is not a man properly judged
by the company he keeps?

❖

To the bride and groom:
May they have a lifetime of love
and an eternity of happiness.

❖

To you on your anniversary:
May every new day bring more
happiness than yesterday.

❖

Do not let your heart grow old
Though birthdays come and go;
To the youthful thoughts keep hold
Then, happiness you will know.
Happy Birthday.

✤

May you live to be a hundred years
With one extra year to repent.
    —*Traditional Irish Toast*

✤

Let your boat of life be light
Packed with only what you need—
A homely home and simple pleasures,
One or two friends, worth the name,
Someone to love and someone to love you,
A cat, a dog, and a pipe or two,
Enough to eat and enough to wear,
And a little more than enough to drink...
For thirst is a dangerous thing.
    —*Jerome K. Jerome, Three Men in a Boat*

✤

May good luck
be always your friend
Through life in all that you do
And may trouble be always
a stranger to you.

❖

Bless your little
Irish heart
and every other Irish part.

❖

Here's to the health
of your enemies' enemies!

❖

May the dust of your carriage wheels
Blind the eyes of your foes.

❖

May the roof above
you never fall in,
And your friends gathered below
never fall out.

❖

The Irish Toast
"Slainte" (slauntca)—Cheers (health)

❖

A Toast for an Irish Bachelor
May you have nicer legs
than yours under the table
before the new spuds are up.

❖

We drink to your coffin,
May it be built
from the wood
Of a hundred-year-old
oak tree
That I shall plant tomorrow.

❖

I drink to myself
and one other
And may that one other
be he
Who drinks to himself and one other
and may that one other be me!

❖

May you live all the
Days of your life.

❖

Wishing you always:
Walls for the wind,
And a roof for the rain,
And tea beside the fire.
Laughter to cheer you.
And those you love near you,
And all that your heart might desire.

❖

May the light of heaven shine
On your grace.

❖

"Slainthe Is Saul Agat" (slawne-cheh-iss sole-agat)—
Health and life to you!

❖

May you die in bed aged one hundred years
Shot by a jealous husband.

❖

May you live as long as you want
And never want as long as you live.

❖

Here's to health to thine and thee
Not forgetting mine and me
When thine and thee next meet mine and me
May mine and me have as much welcome for
thine and thee
As thine and thee have had for mine and me
tonight.

❖

May your doctor never earn a penny out of you
May your heart never give out
May the ten toes of your feet steer you clear of
all misfortune
And before you're much older
May you hear much better toasts than this.

❖

May the frost never afflict your spuds
May the outside leaves of your cabbage always
be free from worm
May the crows never pick at your haystack
And may your ass always be in foal.

❖

May you be poor in misfortune
Rich in blessings
Slow to make enemies
Quick to make friends
But rich or poor
Quick or slow
May you know nothing but happiness
From this day forth.

❖

May the wind be always at your back, especially coming home on Saturday night.

❖

May St. Peter never ask you to light a fire on a lake or advise a headstrong woman.

❖

May you always keep out from the priests; that way you will keep in with them.

❖

May you never stay seeing the bees without spotting the honey.

❖

May you dance with all the saints in heaven bar St. Vitus.

❖

May you be as well as you can bear to be.

❖

May the hand that offers trouble be as idle as the left hand of a bodhran.

❖

May the lips that speak ill of you never say thanks to St. Peter.

❖

May your horse always stand in the middle of the fair.

❖

Let your enemies hear the bees but may you get the honey.

❖

May you get what you're after with the help of God and two policemen.

❖

Hold your hour and have another!

❖

Wet your whistle well and may we never die of the drought!

❖

Here's your health for consideration!

❖

Drink up! It's always the next one that sickens you.

❖

Good luck whatever!

❖

Good health without a cold in your pipes!

❖

Here's one for the road and may you know every
turning!

❖

Here's mud in one eye and a glint in the other!

❖

May the next drop make the grass grow long on the
road to hell for you!

❖

Here's to the same again or something similar!

❖

Good luck to you and bad shoes to your advisers.
(Said to a drinking companion who complains about
drink being bad for a man.)

❖

Health! May your well never run dry!

❖

Peace on your hand!

❖

May God never knock you down as long as you keep
putting them up!

❖

I'll give you your health and may your enemies be beggars!

❖

The face of the sad story be turned away from us!

❖

Your life and your health to you!

❖

Health to the man who buys his round
To heaven's alehouses be he bound.

❖

Drink as if it was your last one but may the last one not come till morning.

❖

May God hold you in the hollow of His hand and have a drink in the other for you.

❖

May we keep a little of the fuel of youth to warm our body in old age.

❖

May you live to be a hundred—and decide the rest for yourself.

❖

You're not as young as you used to be
But you're not as old as you're going to be
So watch it!

❖

Here is to loving, to romance, to us.
May we travel together through time.
We alone count as none, but together we're one,
For our partnership puts love to rhyme.

❖

A generation of children on the children of your children.

❖

May he/she grow twice as tall as yourself and half as wise.

❖

May poverty always be a day's march behind us.

❖

May the sunshine of comfort dispel the clouds of despair.

❖

Here's to you! No matter how old you are, you don't look it!

❖

Many happy returns of the day of your birth;
Many blessings to brighten your pathway on earth;
Many friendships to cheer and provoke you to mirth;
Many feastings and frolics to add to your girth.
—*Robert H. Lord*

❖

A Christmas wish—
May you never forget
what is worth remembering
or remember
what is best forgotten.

❖

Holly and ivy hanging up
And something wet in every cup.

❖

May you be as contented as Christmas finds you all the
year round.

❖

May you be the first house in the parish to welcome
St. Nicholas.

❖

May your corn stand high as yourself, your fields grow
bigger with rain, and the mare know its own way home
on Christmas night.

❖

May your sheep all have lambs
but not on Christmas night.

❖

Peace and plenty for many a Christmas to come.

❖

Friendship's the wine of life.
Let's drink of it and to it.

❖

Here's all that's fine to you!
Books and old wine to you!
Girls be divine to you!
—*Richard Hovey*

❖

Here's to a friend. He knows you well and likes you
just the same.

❖

To our best friends, who know the worst about us but refuse to believe it.

❖

May the clouds in your life form only a background for a lovely sunset.

❖

May we be happy and our enemies know it.

❖

May we never feel want, nor ever want feeling.

❖

May you always distinguish between the weeds and the flowers.
May you be merry and lack nothing.
—*Shakespeare*

❖

May the good Lord take a liking to you—but not too soon.

❖

May the holy saints be about your bed, and about your board, from this time to the latter end—God help us all!

❖

The health of the salmon to you:
a long life,
a full heart,
and a wet mouth!

❖

May the path to hell grow green
for lack of travelers.

❖

May the rocks in your field turn to gold.

❖

May time never turn your head gray.

❖

May you be seven times better off a year from now.

❖

May your fire never go out.

❖

May your well never run dry.

❖

To a full moon on a dark night
And the road downhill all the way to your door.

❖

To a warm bed, a dry stool, and glass in your window.

❖

To the thirst that is yet to come.

❖

Here's to love and unity,
Dark corners and opportunity.

❖

Here's to love, which begins with a fever and ends with
a yawn.

❖

Here's to you who halves my sorrows and doubles my
joys.

❖

Let's drink to love,
Which is nothing—
Unless it's divided by two.

❖

May love draw the curtain and friendship the cork.

❖

May we kiss those we please
And please those we kiss.

❖

May we love as long as we live, and live as long as we
love.

❖

As we start the New Year,
Let's get down on our knees
to thank God we're on our feet.

❖

In the New Year,
may your right hand always be stretched out in friendship, but never in want.

❖

May the New Year bring summer in its wake.

❖

Fat cattle, green fields, and many a bushel in your
barn.

❖

To the good old days...we weren't so good, 'cause we weren't so old!

❖

May the Irish hills caress you.
May her lakes and rivers bless you.
May the luck of the Irish enfold you.
May the blessings of St. Patrick behold you.

❖

May the leprechauns be near you to spread luck along your way
And may all the Irish angels smile upon you on St. Pat's Day.

❖

Here's to you,
And here's to me;
But as you're not here,
Here's two to me.

❖

May you have many children
and may they grow as mature in taste
and healthy in color
and as sought after
as the contents of this glass.

❖

A good wife and health
Are a man's best wealth.

THE TRIADS
OF
IRELAND

Three worst smiles:
 the smile of a wave,
 the smile of a loose woman,
 the grin of a dog ready to leap.

Three things that are best in the world:
 the hand of a good carpenter,
 the hand of a skilled woman,
 the hand of a good smith.

The three wealths of fortunate people:
 a ready conveyance,
 ale without a habitation,
 a safeguard upon the road.

Three sons whom chastity bears to wisdom:
 valor,
 generosity,
 laughter.

Three entertainers of a gathering:
 a jester,
 a juggler,
 a lapdog.

Three rejoicings followed by sorrow:
 a wooer's,
 a thief's,
 a talebearer's.

Three things best for a chief:
 justice,
 peace,
 an army.

Three worst things for a chief:
 sloth,
 treachery,
 evil counsel.

Three rejoicings that are worse than sorrow:
 the joy of a man who has defrauded another,
 the joy of a man who has perjured himself,
 the joy of a man who has slain his brother in contesting
his land.

The three things that ruin wisdom:
 ignorance,
 inaccurate knowledge,
 forgetfulness.

Three nurses of dignity:
 a fine figure,
 a good memory,
 piety.

Three dark things of the world:
 giving a thing into keeping,
 guaranteeing,
 fostering.

Three unfortunate things for a householder:
 proposing to a bad woman,
 serving a bad chief,
 exchanging for bad land.

Three excellent things for a householder:
 proposing to a good woman,
 serving a good chief,
 exchanging for good land.

Three that are most difficult to talk to:
 a king about his booty,
 a Viking in his hauberk,
 a boor who's under patronage.

Three whose spirits are highest:
a young scholar after having read his psalms,
a youngster who has put on a man's attire,
a maiden who has been made a woman.

Three things which justice demands:
judgment,
measure,
conscience.

Three things which judgment demands:
wisdom,
penetration,
knowledge.

Three wealths in barren places:
a well in a mountain,
fire out of a stone,
wealth in the possession of a hard man.

Three renovators of the world:
the woman of a woman,
a cow's udder,
a smith's molding block.

Three things for which an enemy is loved:
wealth,
beauty,
worth.

Three things for which a friend is hated:
trespassing,
keeping aloof,
fecklessness.

Three concealments upon which forfeiture does not close:
a wife's dowry,
the food of a married couple,
a boy's foster fee.

Three contracts that are reversed by the decision of a judge:
the contracts of a woman,
of a son,
of a cotter.

Three rude ones of the world:
a youngster mocking an old man,
a healthy person mocking an invalid,
a wise man mocking a fool.

Three that are incapable of special contracts:
a son whose father is alive,
a betrothed woman,
the serf of a chief.

Three sons that do not share inheritance:
a son begotten in a brake,
the son of a slave,
the son of a girl still wearing tresses.

Three sparks that kindle love:
a face,
demeanor,
speech.

Three chains by which evil propensity is bound:
a covenant,
a monastic rule,
law.

The rocks to which lawful behavior is tied:
a monastery,
a chieftain,
the family.

Three deposits with usufruct:
depositing a woman,
a horse,
salt.

Three candles that illumine every darkness:
truth,
nature,
knowledge.

Three glories of the gathering:
a beautiful wife,
a good horse,
a swift hound.

Three things that constitute a king:
a contract with other kings,
the feast of Tar,
abundance during his reign.

Three ungentlemanly things:
interrupting stories,
a mischievous game,
jesting so as to raise a blush.

Three locks that lock up secrets:
shame,
silence,
closeness.

Three smiles that are worse than sorrow:
the smile of the snow as it melts,
the smile of your wife on you after another man has
been with her,
the grin of a hound ready to leap at you.

Three keys that unlock thoughts:
drunkenness,
trustfulness,
love.

Three fewnesses that are better than plenty:
a fewness of fine words,
a fewness of cows in grass,
a fewness of friends around ale.

Three inheritances that are divided in the presence of
heirs:
the inheritance of a jester,
of a madman,
of an old man.

Three ruins of a tribe:
a lying chief,
a false judge,
a lustful priest.

Three youthful sisters:
desire,
beauty,
generosity.

Three aged sisters:
groaning,
chastity,
ugliness.

Three well-bred sisters:
constancy,
well-spokenness,
kindliness.

Three ill-bred sisters:
fierceness,
lustfulness,
obduracy.

Three preparations of a good man's house:
ale,
a bath,
a large fire.

Three characteristics of obstinacy:
long visits,
staring,
constant questioning.

Three sisters of good fortune:
good breeding,
liberality,
mirth.

The three chief sins:
avarice,
gluttony,
lust.

Three sisters of good repute:
diligence,
prudence,
bountifulness.

Three sisters of ill repute:
  inertness,
  grudging,
  closefistedness.

Three things that constitute a harper:
  a tune to make you cry,
  a tune to make you laugh,
  a tune to put you to sleep.

Three angry sisters:
  blasphemy,
  strife,
  foulmouthedness.

Three irreverent sisters:
  usefulness,
  an easy bearing,
  firmness.

Three sounds of increase:
  the lowing of a cow in milk,
  the din of a smithy,
  the swish of a plow.

Three causes that do not die with neglect:
the causes of an imbecile,
of oppression,
of ignorance.

Three bloodsheds that need not be impugned:
the bloodshed of battle,
of jealousy,
of mediating.

Three things by which every angry person is known:
an outburst of passion,
trembling,
growing pale.

Three things that characterize every patient person:
repose,
silence,
blushing.

Three cohabitations that do not pay a marriage-portion:
taking her by force,
outraging her without her knowledge through drunkenness,
her being violated by a king.

Three that are not entitled to exemption:
restoring a son,
the tools of an artificer,
hostageship.

Three signs of folly:
contention,
wrangling,
attachment to everybody.

Three deposits that need not be returned:
the deposits of an imbecile,
of a high dignitary,
a fixed deposit.

Three dead ones that are paid for with living things:
an apple tree,
a hazel bush,
a sacred grove.

Three things that make a fool wise:
learning,
steadiness,
docility.

Three things that neither swear nor are sworn:
a woman,
a son who does not support his father,
a dumb person.

Three things that make a wise man foolish:
quarreling,
anger,
drunkenness.

Three that are not entitled to renunciation of authority:
a son and his father,
a wife and her husband,
a serf and his lord.

Three things that show every good man:
a special gift,
valor,
piety.

Three things that show a bad man:
bitterness,
hatred,
cowardice.

Three who do not adjudicate though they are possessed
of wisdom:
 a man who sues,
 a man who is being sued,
 a man who is bribed to give judgment.

Three on whom acknowledgment does not fall in its
time:
 death,
 ignorance,
 carelessness.

Three great rushes:
 the rush of water,
 the rush of fire,
 the rush of falsehood.

Three maidens that bring hatred upon misfortune:
 talking,
 laziness,
 insincerity.

Three maidens that bring love to good fortune:
 silence,
 diligence,
 sincerity.

Three woman-days:
 Monday,
 Tuesday,
 Wednesday.

Three man-days:
 Thursday,
 Friday,
 Sunday.

Three hateful things in speech:
 stiffness,
 obscurity,
 a bad delivery.

The three finest sights in the world:
 a field of ripe wheat,
 a ship in full sail,
 the wife of a MacDonnell with child.

Three things that are undignified for everyone:
 driving one's horse before one's lord so as to soil his dress,
 going to speak to him without being summoned,
 staring in his face as he is eating his food.

Three steadinesses of good womanhood:
 keeping a steady tongue,
 a steady chastity,
 a steady housewifery.

Three welcomes of an alehouse:
 plenty,
 kindliness,
 art.

Three prohibitions of food:
 to eat it without giving thanks,
 to eat it before its proper time,
 to eat it after a guest.

Three excellences of dress:
 elegance,
 comfort,
 lastingness.

Three indications of a dignity in a person:
 a fine figure,
 a fine bearing,
 eloquence.

Three that are not entitled to sick-maintenance:
 a man who absconds from his chief,
 from his family,
 from his poet.

Three coffers whose depth is not known:
 the coffer of a chieftain,
 of the Church,
 of a privileged poet.

Three disagreeable things at home:
 a scolding wife,
 a squalling child,
 a smoky chimney.

NOTES AND RECIPES

ABOUT THE AUTHOR

Ray Foley has been a bartender for more than twenty years. He is the publisher of *Bartender* magazine and the author of *Bartending for Dummies, The Ultimate Little Martini Book*, and *The Ultimate Little Shooter Book*. He has appeared on *Good Morning America, Live with Regis and Kathie Lee,* and countless other shows. Ray resides in New Jersey with his wife and partner, Jaclyn.